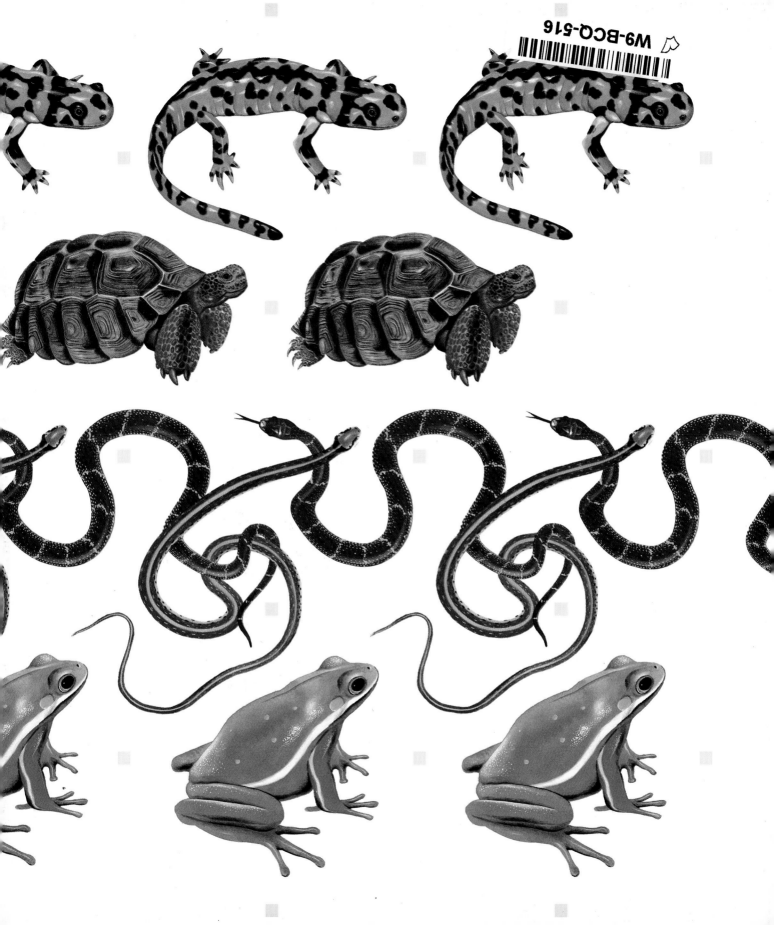

Poison Ivy and Poison Oak

This weed (shown above) causes an itchy rash if you touch it. Poison Ivy grows like a vine, and Poison Oak grows like a shrub. Try to remember what the leaves look like, and take care when walking in the country. If you do touch it, washing the area may reduce the itching. Your local drug store will have various remedies that will help.

Animal Sizes

One of these symbols is shown with each animal. It shows you at a glance how big the animal is likely to be. All measurements describe the length of the animal from the tip of its nose to the end of its tail.

Up to 2 ins   **2–5 ins**

5–12 ins

Over 12 ins

For snakes, the measurements are shown on the symbol below, also from the tip of the snake's nose to the end of its tail.

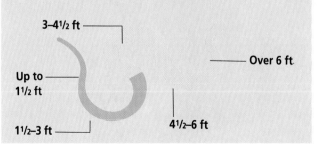

3–4½ ft

Over 6 ft

Up to 1½ ft

1½–3 ft   4½–6 ft

SCIENCE NATURE GUIDES

AMPHIBIANS & REPTILES
OF NORTH AMERICA

Christiane Gunzi

ILLUSTRATIONS BY
Alan Male

THUNDER BAY
P·R·E·S·S

Conservation

Every animal is closely linked to its surroundings. It feeds on other animals or plants and it makes its nest or den in trees, among rocks, or bushes, or under the ground. Many animals prefer particular kinds of climate and landscape. As you learn more about a habitat, you will get to know which plants and animals you can expect to find there.

Hundreds of years ago, many more wild animals used to live in North America, but many of their habitats have been damaged or destroyed by agriculture, industry and the pollution that both of these cause. Some wild animals are in danger of disappearing altogether. These animals are often protected by federal law, or by state laws.

On page 78, you will find the names of some organizations who campaign for the protection of particular animals and habitats. By joining them and supporting their efforts, you can help to preserve our animals and their habitats.

Countryside Code

1 **Always go collecting with a friend,** and always tell an adult where you have gone.
2 **Leave any wild animals that you find alone**—they may attack you if frightened.
3 **Leave their nests or dens untouched**.
4 **Keep your dog under control**.
5 **Ask permission** before exploring or crossing private property.
6 **Keep to footpaths** as much as possible.
7 **Leave fence gates as you find them.**
8 **Wear long pants, shoes and a long-sleeved shirt** in deer tick country.
9 **Ask your parents not to light fires** except in fireplaces in special picnic areas.

Thunder Bay Press
5880 Oberlin Drive
Suite 400
San Diego, CA 92121

First published in the United States
by Thunder Bay Press, 1995

© Dragon's World, 1995
© Text Dragon's World, 1995
© Species and habitat illustrations
  Alan Male, 1995
© Other illustrations Dragon's World, 1995

Habitat paintings by Alan Male.
Headbands by Antonia Phillips.
Identification and activities illustrations by
Mr Gay Galsworthy.

Editor	Diana Briscoe
Designer	James Lawrence
Design Assistants	Karen Ferguson
	Victoria Furbisher
Art Director	John Strange
Editorial Director	Pippa Rubinstein

Complete Cataloging in Publication (CIP) is available through the Library of Congress. LC Card Number:

Printed in Italy

ISBN 1–57145–020–3

Contents

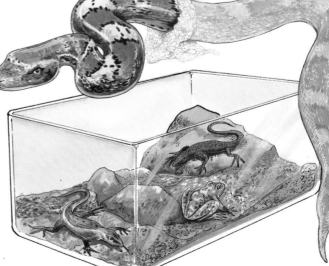

What's the Difference?

Amphibians and reptiles have lived on Earth for hundreds of millions of years, and today there are at least 4,000 kinds of amphibian and 6,700 kinds of reptile. Many more have become extinct (died out) since the first amphibian crawled out of the sea about 360 million years ago. Reptiles appeared about 10,000,000 years later, but only became the dominant animal group about 285 million years ago. The dinosaurs were all reptiles.

This book shows you how and where to look for these fascinating animals, and what you can expect to see in different habitats at different times of day. You will discover what makes an amphibian different from a reptile, what these animals like to eat, and how many young they have. The scientific study of amphibians and reptiles is called herpetology. If one day you are an expert, you will be a herpetologist.

An amphibian's life cycle

Most amphibians breed in or near water and the males often call to attract the females. Some female amphibians lay a mass of eggs in water, others lay one egg at a time, attached to a water plant. The eggs hatch after a few hours, or days, or even weeks.

The young hatchlings are called larvae. They take from between a few days to several months to develop into adults and climb onto land. Some kinds of amphibian never change into an adult form, but stay as larvae living in water for their whole life.

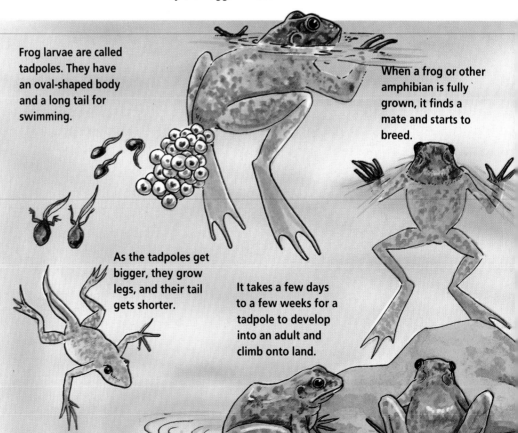

Frogs breed in or near water. The males call to attract the females. The females lay their eggs in water.

Frog larvae are called tadpoles. They have an oval-shaped body and a long tail for swimming.

When a frog or other amphibian is fully grown, it finds a mate and starts to breed.

As the tadpoles get bigger, they grow legs, and their tail gets shorter.

It takes a few days to a few weeks for a tadpole to develop into an adult and climb onto land.

How to use this book

To identify an animal that you do not recognize—for example, the salamander and lizard shown here—follow these steps.

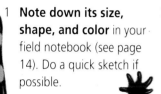

1 **Note down its size, shape, and color** in your field notebook (see page 14). Do a quick sketch if possible.

2 **Look if the animal has any special features,** such as spiky scales, claws, or webbed toes (pages 6–7 show you what to look for to tell amphibians and reptiles apart).

3 **Decide which habitat you are in.** The descriptions at the beginning of each section will help you. Each habitat has a different picture band (see below on this page).

4 **Look through the pages with that habitat picture band.** The picture and information with each animal will help you to identify it. This Spotted Salamander (left) is an amphibian that belongs to the Mole Salamander family (see page 21).

5 **If you cannot find the animal there,** look through the other sections. This Collared Lizard (see above and page 58) is a reptile that belongs to the Iguanid family.

6 **If you cannot find it in this book,** it may be very rare. Try looking in other books on amphibians and reptiles (see page 79 for suggestions).

A reptile's life cycle

Some reptiles lay eggs, and others give birth to miniature versions of themselves. Many egg-laying reptiles lay their eggs in a hole dug in the sand or under a rock or leaves, then leave them. Others, such as some snakes, lizards, and alligators, stay with their eggs and keep them warm until they hatch. Some kinds of lizards and snakes give birth to fully formed young.

Top-of-page picture bands

This book is divided into different habitats. Each habitat has a different picture band at the top of the page. These are shown below.

Backyards & Parks

Forests & Woodlands

Streams & Rivers

Lakes, Ponds, & Marshes

Prairies & Grasslands

Deserts & Arid Scrub

Reptile or Amphibian?

When you are trying to identify a reptile or an amphibian, look at the animal's shape, skin texture, feet, and color.
- Is the skin scaly or smooth?
- Do the feet have claws or webbing?

It is quite easy to confuse an amphibian—such as a salamander—with a reptile like a lizard. But once you know which clues to look for, you will soon be able to spot the difference between one group of animals and another.

Parts of an amphibian

Sacral hump

Warts on skin

Bulging eyes

Round ear drum (tympanum)

Webbed feet

Parts of a reptile

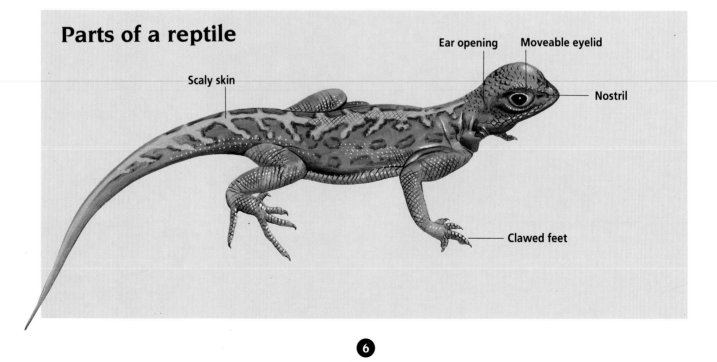

Ear opening

Moveable eyelid

Scaly skin

Nostril

Clawed feet

Skin, scales & scutes

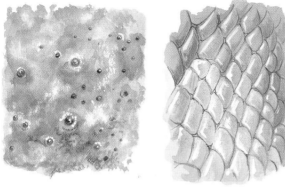

Amphibian   Reptile

Amphibians have moist skin without scales. Sometimes their skin is smooth and sometimes rough, but never scaly. Reptiles always have tough, scaly skin, and sometimes the scales are spiky too. Tortoises, turtles, and terrapins have a shell consisting of hard scutes to protect their body.

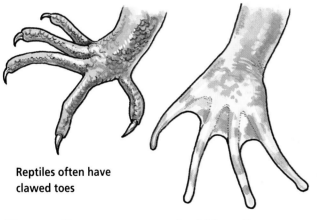

Reptiles often have clawed toes

Feet & toes

Amphibians often have webbed feet

Reptiles often have clawed toes, but amphibians do not. Many amphibians have webbed toes – true frogs always have webbed toes, tree frogs have toe pads and webbing. Toads have no webbing, and Spadefoot Toads have a special spur on their back foot for digging.

SAFETY FIRST

When you go searching for amphibians or reptiles in the wild, be very cautious. **Don't try to pick up what you find**, because some animals bite. See page 40 for what to do if you are bitten by a snake.

Many amphibians and reptiles like to hide under rocks, dead leaves, and rotten logs, including poisonous snakes. If disturbed, they will try to escape as quickly as possible, but they may try to attack you first. **So, don't take risks.** Never move rocks or logs with your bare hands. It is much safer to use a stick or a boot to gently move logs, leaves, or rocks aside. Wear boots or trainers, and long pants, for your expeditions (see page 14).

Body shape & color

The color and pattern of amphibians and reptiles often varies depending on the age of the animal. Sometimes adults are a completely different color from the young. Frogs are usually slim-bodied, and toads are more squat in shape. Most lizards have tails, sometimes longer than the body. Even snakes have tails, though it is hard to tell where the tail starts because they have no legs.

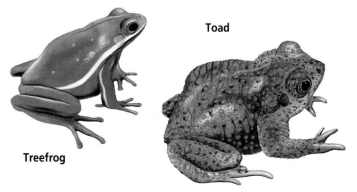

Toad

Treefrog

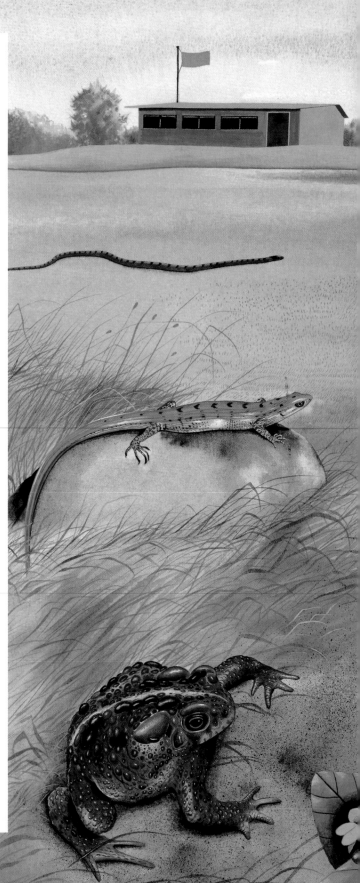

Backyards & Parks

The variety of animals that you are likely to see in your backyard depends on where you live, because reptiles and amphibians usually visit from surrounding areas of meadow, woodland, or another habitat. The most common backyard visitors are those that prefer a mixed habitat.

Backyard reptiles and amphibians have to put up with people constantly disturbing their habitat, by gardening for example. Frogs, toads, lungless salamanders, and some small snakes are the most familiar sights. They usually live under rocks, logs, among garden shrubs, and around garbage and compost heaps. Frogs living in built-up areas may depend on your pond for breeding.

If you want to encourage these animals into your backyard, try to leave an area to grow wild. You may be lucky enough to attract Box Turtles and Hognose Snakes if you have an undisturbed corner of the garden. Trees, shrubs, sheds, and walls provide good hiding places and hunting grounds for lizards, frogs, and some small snakes, too. Some common backyard reptiles, including Brown Snakes, are so are secretive and shy that, unless you are very observant, you may never even know they share your backyard.

This picture shows five reptiles and amphibians from this book. How many do you recognize?

American Toad, Northern Leopard Frog, Common Garter Snake, Southern Alligator Lizard, Brown Snake

Backyards & Parks

Fowler's Toad

Fowler's Toad is usually yellow, greenish, or brown, with blotches on its back. It looks similar to the American Toad, but it has more warts in each of the largest dark spots, and there are no spots on its belly. You are most likely to see this toad in the evening when it is searching for insects. During the day it usually stays in its burrow. Fowler's Toads live in most of the eastern U.S. South of New England, especially in backyards and wooded areas with sandy soil.

Animal group: Amphibian
Family: True toad
Size: 2–3 ins
Eats insects and other small invertebrates

American Toad

You can find this big, knobbly toad in most of the eastern U.S. and Canada. The American Toad is usually brown, dull red, or olive with a spotted belly, and covered with orange or brown warts. It has big, bony crests above each eye and sometimes a light stripe down the middle of its back. This toad likes to live in damp places from backyards to mountain forests where there are lots of insects to eat. It is most active at night, and you can hear its musical call in the springtime.

Animal group: Amphibian
Family: True toad
Size: 2–3½ ins
Eats insects and other small invertebrates

Northern Leopard Frog

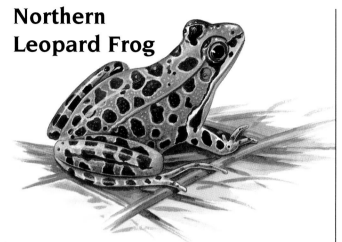

You can easily recognize this slim-bodied frog by its leopardlike round, dark spots with light edges. Northern Leopard Frogs live all over the northern U.S. except for the West Coast. They especially like wet, grassy fields, meadows, and marshes. Look out for one hopping along in a zig-zag pattern as it heads for water. Listen at night for the Leopard Frog's call, a long, rattling snore.

Animal group: Amphibian
Family: True frog
Size: 2–5 ins
Eats insects and other small invertebrates

Squirrel Treefrog

This little frog changes colour easily from green to brown, sometimes with spots or yellow marks on its back. It may also have a dark mark between its eyes. Squirrel Treefrogs like all kinds of habitats as long as it is wet. You can often hear their ducklike calls after summer rain showers. These frogs are very busy at night, and often come near to houses to catch moths and other insects. During the day, they prefer to hide among garden shrubs, sometimes in large groups. They are most common along the southeastern coast.

Animal group: Amphibian
Family: Treefrog
Size: 1-1³/₄ ins
Eats insects

Woodhouse's Toad

This toad lives in many habitats throughout the Midwest and West, including backyards, desert streams, marshes, and rain puddles. You are most likely to see one at night, when it is out and about catching insects. It is usually yellow, greenish, or brown, with a light stripe on its back and dark warts on its skin. There are two bony crests above its eyes. Listen for this toad's call, like a lamb bleating.

Animal group: Amphibian
Family: True toad
Size: 2–4 ins
Eats insects and other small invertebrates

Eastern Hognose Snake

This plump snake is named after its piglike snout. It can be various colors from yellow to brown to gray, and is usually spotted. The Eastern Hognose Snake has a curious way of defending itself, which has earned it nicknames such as "Puff Adder" and "Blow Viper." If it is disturbed, the snake puffs out its body, spreads its neck, hisses, then strikes at the intruder. This makes the snake look bigger and more threatening than it really is. If this performance does not work, the snake turns over and lays very still with its tongue hanging out, pretending to be dead. The female lays up to 61 eggs in a shallow hole in summer.

Animal group: Reptile
Family: Colubrid snake – Size: 20–45 ins
Eats frogs and toads, and also crickets and other insects

Common Garter Snake

You can find these snakes all over the U.S. and Canada in parks, meadows, woodlands, and yards. They usually live close to ponds, streams, and marshes, where there is plenty of moisture, so look for one as it searches for food during the day. Common Garter Snakes may be many shades of green, yellowish, or gray, but they nearly always have three yellowish stripes along their back and sides. These snakes mate in spring, and the females give birth to up to 85 young in late summer to fall.

Animal group: Reptile
Family: Colubrid snake
Size: 8–26 ins
Eats frogs, toads, salamanders, earthworms, and sometimes mice and small fish

Southern Alligator Lizard

This long, shiny lizard has short legs and moves very stiffly because its hard scales act like a suit of armor. It is usually red-brown to yellowish gray, with yellow eyes and dark bands on its back and tail. Look on bushes in open forests where there are oak trees, and you may see one of these lizards using its tail to cling to twigs and branches as it climbs. The female lays about twelve eggs during the warmest months of the year.

Animal group: Reptile – Family: Anguid lizard – Size: 6–15 ins
Hunts for insects, spiders, and scorpions, but will eat any animal small enough to overpower

Eastern Box Turtle

This pretty turtle has a hinged lower shell that shuts snugly against the upper shell when the turtle needs to hide. Eastern Box Turtles are usually brown, patterned with orange or yellow blotches. The males have red eyes and the females have yellowish brown eyes. These turtles like wet meadows, forests, and fields. Look for them in the early morning or after a summer shower, when they come out to search for their favorite foods of slugs and strawberries. These turtles can live for more than a hundred years. They are land turtles, but they sometimes like to soak in mud or water. In hot, dry weather, they burrow under a log for shelter. The female lays eggs in a hole that she digs in the soil.

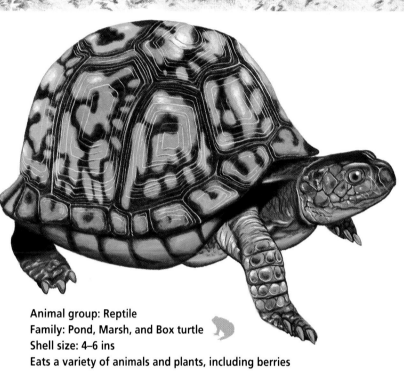

Animal group: Reptile
Family: Pond, Marsh, and Box turtle
Shell size: 4–6 ins
Eats a variety of animals and plants, including berries

Eastern Fence Lizard

Often called the "Pine lizard", this lizard can be gray, brown, or rust-colored. The female has dark lines across her back, and the male has a blue throat. Look for these lizards in sunny places on walls, fences, and logs and tree stumps. When surprised, the Eastern Fence Lizard will dash up a tree or wall, then stop suddenly and stay absolutely still.

Animal group: Reptile
Family: Iguanid lizard
Size: 3 1/2–7 1/2 ins
Eats all kinds of insects and other invertebrates, especially beetles

Brown Snake

These small, secretive snakes used to be a common sight in city parks and vacant lots, but they are less common today because of development. They are usually gray or yellowish brown, with two rows of small dark spots and a wide light stripe. The young have a yellowish collar around the neck. Brown Snakes like damp places, and hide under logs, rocks, or even trash. They often gather together in groups to hibernate in the fall. These snakes give birth to up to thirty young in June to September.

Animal group: Reptile
Family: Colubrid snake
Size: 9–13 ins
Eats earthworms, slugs, and snails

Looking For Species

Most reptiles and amphibians are afraid of people and live secretive lives. To be successful in finding and watching them, you will need plenty of enthusiasm and patience. Like bird watching, you will improve greatly with practice. When you first go out searching, you may not find anything, but you will find once you learn where to look.

A good way to start is to join a local wildlife group or visit pet shops, zoos and vivariums near you to find out which species are common in your area. Never go alone, always take a friend.

Equipment

You do not need any special equipment. However, sharp eyes are important! A pair of binoculars and a camera are also useful. Take your field notebook, plus pens and pencils to make notes. Read the Conservation and Safety Code (page 2) before you go. You must wear stout shoes or boots if you are walking through brush or undergrowth where there may be snakes. Wear long pants and a long-sleeved top if you are in deer tick country.

Keeping records

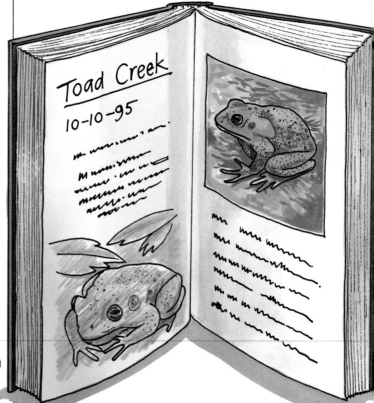

Making notes in your field notebook is an excellent way to learn from your observations. Your notes and photos will help you identify the animals.

1 **Give a name to each new site that you visit.** Write down the date and what sort of habitat it is (pond, garden, field etc.)
2 **Each time you visit that site, record what the weather was like** and what time of day it was.
3 **When you find a reptile or amphibian, watch it carefully.** Make a note of its shape, color and size to help identification.
4 **Take a photograph if you can!** If you approach quietly, many species will stay still. Note the photo number and what it was. Then you can tell which is which when they are developed.
5 **Write down what the animal was doing (sleeping, eating, etc.,)** how many there were, and what noise it was making.

Catching & handling

DO NOT APPROACH OR TRY TO CATCH ANY SNAKE unless told by an adult expert that it is safe to do so. Only 17 out of more than 100 species in North America, are poisonous but some of these are very dangerous. See page 40 for what to do if you are bitten by a snake. If you can, visit a vivarium where you can learn to safely handle a snake.

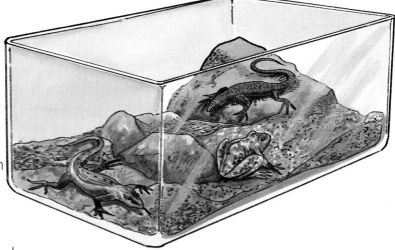

Although most lizards and turtles are harmless, they are best left alone. Watch them quietly instead. If you grab a lizard by the tail or frighten it badly, it may "lose" its tail. Large lizards and some turtles can give you a nasty bite. There are only two species of poisonous lizard, the large Gila Monster and the Mexican beaded lizard.

You may be able to catch newts, young salamanders, frogs or toads using a dip net in a pond. Most salamanders, newts and frogs can be safely handled. But remember, amphibians are "cold-blooded" and have soft, moist skins. They do not like being held in warm, dry hands. Instead tip them into a small plastic aquarium with some damp vegetation. When you have finished looking at them, put them back where you found them.

Some toads and salamanders can secrete an unpleasant liquid from their skins. This can cause swelling and discomfort if it enters a cut or gets in your mouth or eyes. Rinse your eyes or mouth thoroughly with clean water if this happens.

Adopt a site

If you have a favorite pond, wood or field near you, visit it regularly (perhaps once a month) and get to know it really well. You will be able to find out

- **Which animals live there**, and which are just passing through?
- **What happens in winter and in spring?**
- **Make a plan of the site,** name the different parts and mark on where the animals are found. You could repeat this four times a year.

Forests & Woodlands

Damp, shady forests and woodlands make an ideal habitat for amphibians that need to keep their skin cool and moist, such as salamanders and frogs.

The main types of forest in North America are evergreen forests and broad-leaved, deciduous woodlands. An evergreen forest may contain pine, fir, and spruce trees, which have needle leaves and are "coniferous"—the trees produce cones. In these forests, summers are hot and winters are cold and snowy.

In the broad-leaved woodlands of North America, there are oak, maple, beech, and elm trees among others. These trees form a thick canopy of leaves in summer, and lose their leaves in winter, forming a dense layer of leaf litter on the forest floor. This leaf litter provides a good hiding place for salamanders and newts. There are many other places to shelter in a forest, such as under a pile of logs, inside a rotten tree stump, under the bark of a tree, or high up in the trees.

Many forest reptiles are good tree climbers, and Black Rat Snakes, Corn Snakes, and Rubber Boas often climb trees in search of food. Some are well-camouflaged to blend in with the bark or leaves of the trees.

This picture shows six reptiles and amphibians from this book. How many do you recognize?

Wood Frog, Spotted salamander, Broadhead Skink, Ringneck snake, Corn Snake, Red-backed Salamander

Blanchard's Cricket Frog

This tiny frog belongs to the treefrog family but it doesn't like to climb trees. It prefers to stay on the ground, and likes open woodlands or wet, overgrown meadows where it can live close to a slow-moving stream or shallow pool. Its rough skin is usually light brown or gray, and it always has a dark triangle shape between its eyes and a ragged dark stripe on its long hind legs. Listen for its call, a clicking sound.

Animal group: Amphibian
Family: Treefrog
Size: 1/2–1 1/2 ins
Eats insects and other small invertebrates

Pacific Treefrog

The high-pitched, musical call of this frog is a familiar sound along the Pacific coast. It lives in forests and woodlands where there are ponds, ditches, and streams. This is a rough-skinned frog that can change in color from green to dark brown or black, often with dark spots. There is usually a dark stripe running across each eye and a dark triangle between them. Pacific Treefrogs breed from January to early summer and lay their eggs in quiet streams and ponds.

Animal group: Amphibian – Family: Treefrog
Size: 3/4–2 ins – Eats insects and other small invertebrates

Wood Frog

The Wood Frog is pink, brown, or almost black with a dark patch like a mask over its face. These frogs like damp woodland areas and you can find them all over northern North America. This is the only kind of frog that exists North of the Arctic Circle. Wood Frogs breed in early spring and lay masses of eggs in ponds attached to underwater plants. They are usually out and about during the day, and in the cold winter months they hibernate in leaf litter on the woodland floor.

Animal group: Amphibian
Family: True frog
Size: 1 1/2–3 1/4 ins
Eats insects and other small invertebrates

Red Eft

Animal group: Amphibian – Family: Salamandrid
Size: 1/2–3 1/2 ins
WARNING: These newts have a poisonous substance in their skin that makes them taste nasty to predators. It is not dangerous to humans, but if you touch an eft, wash your hands afterwards.

Red Efts are the brightly colored young of Eastern Newts, and they live on land rather than in water. You can see the efts of Red-Spotted Newts in damp woodlands after a shower of rain as they search for their favorite food, small invertebrates. They are orange to reddish brown with orange-red spots on their back. After 2 to 5 years, the efts turn into adults and take to the water in ponds, lakes, and quiet streams. They breed from late winter to early spring, laying 200 to 400 eggs, one at a time, on water plants. The young larvae hatch about 3 to 8 weeks later, and change into efts in late summer or early fall.

Rough-skinned Newt

You can tell this newt apart from others by its very warty skin. It is usually light brown or black on top, with an orange or yellow belly. If threatened, this newt shows off its colorful belly as a warning signal. Rough-skinned Newts live under logs, rocks, and bark in forests along the Pacific coast from California to Alaska. They breed from December to July and from October to November. The female lays her eggs one at a time on water plants, and the young hatch 5 to 10 weeks later. They change into adults when they are 2 to 3 inches long.

Animal group: Amphibian
Family: Salamandrid
Size: 5–8 1/2 ins
Eats insects, slugs, worms, and other small invertebrates
WARNING: This newt produces a poisonous substance in its skin. Wash your hands carefully after you touch it.

Eastern Spadefoot

This is the only spadefoot toad to be found East of the Mississippi River, and you can recognize it by its low, grunting call. A group of these toads makes such a noise that you can hear them up to half a mile away. Most Eastern Spadefoots are olive or brown with red spots, and they usually have two yellowish lines running along the back. Like other spadefoot toads, they are good at digging, and they burrow in the soil for shelter. Their burrows keep them safe from predators and from drought. These toads breed year-round in the South and from early spring to early fall in the North, usually at night following heavy rains. They lay their eggs on pond plants. The tadpoles hatch after two days and change into adults in 2 to 8 weeks.

Animal group: Amphibian – Family: Spadefoot toad
Size: 1 3/4–3 1/4 ins
Eats insects and other small invertebrates
WARNING: Some people are allergic to the substance produced in the skin of spadefoots, so if you touch one, wash your hands afterwards.

Forests & Woodlands

Slimy Salamander

This large, shiny, black salamander is speckled with many small silver or golden spots on its head, back, and tail. It is named after the sticky substance its skin produces to put off predators. Slimy Salamanders breed in spring and fall in the North, and in summer in the South. They lay a clutch of 6 to 36 eggs in a rotten log or underground, and the female guards the nest until the larvae hatch.

Animal group: Amphibian
Family: Lungless salamander – Size: 4½–8½ ins
Hunts at night for small invertebrates on the forest floor
Also found around cave entrances

Ensatina

You can recognize this salamander because its tail is narrow instead of thick at the base. If a predator grabs an Ensatina by its tail, the tail breaks off so the salamander can escape. The tail then regrows a few weeks later, a trick many salamanders use. When threatened, these salamanders arch their tail. The male's tail is often longer than its body. Ensatinas can be all sorts of colors from reddish brown to dark brown, with cream, yellow, or orange spots or blotches. They live in redwood forests, and also pine, cedar, and maple forests. In cold or dry weather, they shelter in animal burrows and among rotten logs and roots. They mate in late spring to early summer and the female lays 7 to 25 eggs underground, and cares for them until they hatch in fall or early winter. These salamanders may live for up to fifteen years in the wild.

Animal group: Amphibian
Family: Lungless salamander
Size: 3–5½ ins
Eats spiders, beetles, crickets, and springtails

Red-backed Salamander

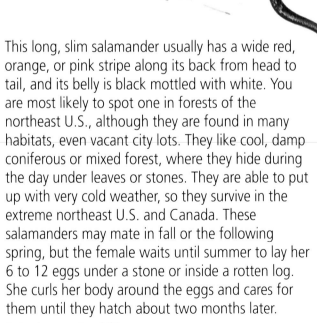

This long, slim salamander usually has a wide red, orange, or pink stripe along its back from head to tail, and its belly is black mottled with white. You are most likely to spot one in forests of the northeast U.S., although they are found in many habitats, even vacant city lots. They like cool, damp coniferous or mixed forest, where they hide during the day under leaves or stones. They are able to put up with very cold weather, so they survive in the extreme northeast U.S. and Canada. These salamanders may mate in fall or the following spring, but the female waits until summer to lay her 6 to 12 eggs under a stone or inside a rotten log. She curls her body around the eggs and cares for them until they hatch about two months later.

Animal group: Amphibian
Family: Lungless salamander
Size: 2½–5 ins
Hunts at night for small insects, slugs, and worms

Spotted Salamander

This pretty salamander spends most of its life hiding underground, so you will be very lucky to see one. It is heavily built, with two rows of yellow or orange spots along its body from head to tail. Spotted Salamanders live in eastern hardwood forests close to water. They breed in spring in the North and earlier in the South. The female lays one or more masses of eggs, which hatch into larvae in 1 to 2 months, and become adults in 2 to 4 months. These salamanders can live for up to twenty years.

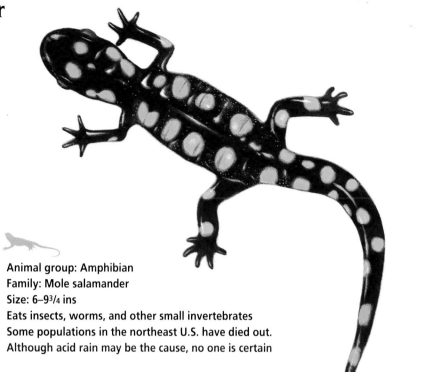

Animal group: Amphibian
Family: Mole salamander
Size: 6–9³/₄ ins
Eats insects, worms, and other small invertebrates
Some populations in the northeast U.S. have died out.
Although acid rain may be the cause, no one is certain

Tiger Salamander

The Tiger Salamander is the largest land salamander in the world. It has a plump body, a wide head, and small eyes. This salamander is often out and about at night after heavy rain hunting for food. These salamanders can be found in many parts of the U.S., not only in forests but also in wet meadows and along streams. They breed in late winter in the southern states and spring and summer in the north, laying their eggs in the temporary pools and streams. The eggs hatch into larvae which turn into adults when they are about 4 inches long.

Animal group: Amphibian
Family: Mole salamander
Size: 6–13 ins
Eats earthworms, insects, small fish, and other amphibians

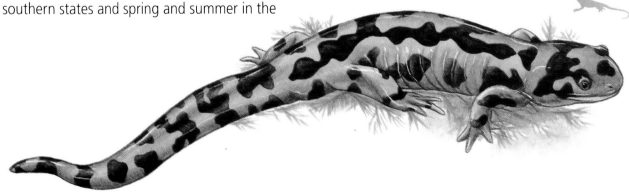

Northern Copperhead

The Copperhead is plump, with reddish brown bands across its body but not on its head. It can be copper, orange, or even pinkish. These snakes like wooded hillsides above streams, where they shelter under rotten logs and large, flat stones. During the day in spring and fall, they bask in the sun, and in the warm summer months they come out at night. They mate in spring or fall and give birth to 2 to 10 live young in late summer or early fall. The young have yellow-tipped tails, which they twitch to attract unsuspecting prey.

Animal group: Reptile
Family: Pit Viper
Size: 22–53 ins
Eats small mice, frogs, lizards, and caterpillars
WARNING: This snake is poisonous and should not be approached

Northern Black Racer

Animal group: Reptile
Family: Colubrid snake
Size: 36–60 ins
Eats large insects, frogs, lizards, other snakes, rodents, and birds

This slender snake has a black, dark blue, brown, or green back, and a lighter belly. It is alert and fast-moving, and speeds away very quickly when it is chased, or even climbs a tree to escape from a predator. When it is cornered, it fights ferociously. Northern Black Racers mate in spring, and the females lay 10 to 25 eggs under a rotten log, a rock, or in a mammal burrow. Sometimes several females lay their eggs in the same place. The young hatch in July to September.

Rubber Boa

This olive green or brown snake looks like a toy snake made of rubber. It is all one color, with large scales on the top of its head and small eyes. It has a short, wide snout and a short blunt tail, so it is difficult to tell which end is which. Rubber Boas live in coniferous forest and damp woodland, where they shelter under rotten logs and in leaf litter. These snakes are good at swimming, burrowing, and climbing, and they use their tail to hold onto branches as they climb. Rubber Boas mate in spring and the females give birth to live young in August to September.

Animal group: Reptile
Family: Boa and Python
Size: 14–33 ins
This snake is a constrictor. It hunts at night for birds, lizards and small mammals

California Slender Salamander

This long-bodied, long-tailed salamander has very short legs and small feet, which makes it easy to recognize. It is usually blackish on top, with a pink, red, or brown band on its back. These salamanders live on the coast and in the central valley of California, especially in redwood forests, where they shelter under logs, bark, and damp leaf litter. They mate in late fall and winter, and the females lay a clutch of four to twenty-one eggs under rocks or logs, often in the same nest.

Animal group: Amphibian
Family: Lungless salamander
Size: 3–5½ ins
Eats small invertebrates

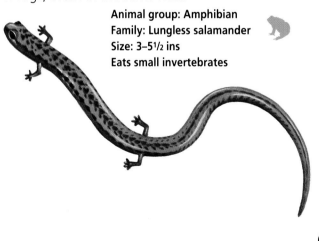

Arboreal Salamander

This yellow-spotted salamander is an excellent tree climber. Look for it on rainy days in oak woodlands near the coast. During the dry summer months, it hides in tree holes and rodent burrows. When it rains, this salamander comes out to hunt for insects in the trees and in leaf litter on the woodland floor. Arboreal Salamanders breed in late spring and early summer, then lay 12 to 24 eggs in a rotten log, a tree, or a hole in the ground. The female cares for the eggs until they hatch one or two months later.

Animal group: Amphibian
Family: Lungless salamander
Size: 4¼–7¼ ins
Feeds on insects and other small invertebrates

Eastern Diamondback Rattlesnake

The Eastern Diamondback is the largest and most dangerous rattlesnake in the U.S. Its bite is so deadly that it can easily kill a human, so if you see one, keep well clear. Rattlesnakes usually rattle their tails to warn away intruders, but not always. The Diamondback Rattlesnake's back is patterned with dark diamonds with light centers. There are also light diagonal lines on each side of its head. These rattlesnakes live in dry oaks and pine forests of the south, sheltering during the day in burrows, beneath stumps and logs, or in thickets of palmetto. They give birth to 7 to 21 young in July to October, each measuring about 12 inches long.

Animal group: Reptile – Family: Pit Viper
Size: 36–72 ins
Feeds on rodents, rabbit-sized mammals, and birds
WARNING: Avoid. Deadly bite

Timber Rattlesnake

This rattlesnake is named for the hardwood forests where it lives. It is sometimes called the "Velvet-tailed Rattler" or "Banded Rattler." It may be yellowish with dark crossbars and a black tail, or almost all black. It comes out during the day from April to October and hunts on warm summer evenings. In northern areas, these snakes gather in large numbers in the fall to hibernate in rocky dens with Copperheads and other snakes. Timber Rattlesnakes can live for up to thirty years in the wild. They mate in late spring or early summer, and give birth to up to a dozen young in fall. Some mate in fall and give birth the following year.

Animal group: Reptile – Family: Pit Viper
Size: 35–74½ ins – Eats rats and mice
WARNING: While not as deadly as the Eastern Diamondback, this snake is dangerously poisonous. Avoid

Black Rat Snake

This big, black, shiny snake is a powerful constrictor. It is an excellent climber and sometimes makes its home in a hole high up in a tree. These snakes look similar to Coachwhips and Black Racers, but they have rougher scales. The Black Rat Snake is found in hardwood forest and bushy areas. It mates in spring and fall, and lays a clutch of 5 to 30 smooth, oblong eggs in a rotten log, leaf litter, or under a rock in June to August. The young hatch several weeks later. These snakes hibernate in winter and often share their den with Timber Rattlesnakes and Copperheads.

Animal group: Reptile
Family: Colubrid snake
Size: 42–72 ins
Eats birds, mice, lizards, small mammals, and also birds' eggs

Corn Snake

This long, beautiful snake of the Southeast is orange, yellow, or gray with large, darker blotches along its back. There is a dark spearpoint mark on the top of its head. This snake's name probably comes from the checkered patterns on its belly, which are similar to the patterns on Indian corn. It is also called the "Red Rat Snake." The Corn Snake is active mainly at night but you may see it in the early evening. It likes wooded groves and rocky hillsides, and climbs trees in search of prey. Corn Snakes mate from March to May, and lay a clutch of 3 to 21 eggs from May to July. The young hatch in July to September.

Animal group: Reptile – Family: Colubrid snake
Size: 24–72 ins – Eats rats, mice, birds, and bats

Ringneck Snake

You cannot mistake this small, slim snake because it has a distinct yellow, orange, or cream ring around its neck. Its back is gray, olive, brown, or black, and it has a bright yellow, red, or orange belly. Ringneck Snakes are shy and hide under flat rocks, logs, and loose tree bark. They are found in moist forests and rocky wooded hillsides. They mate in the spring or fall, and the females lay clutches of 1 to 10 white or yellowish eggs in a nesting site in June to July. After about eight weeks, the young hatch. Ringneck Snakes sometimes twist their tail to show the colorful underside. This has given them the nickname of "Corkscrew Snakes."

Animal group: Reptile
Family: Colubrid snake
Size: 6–15 ins
Eats insects, small salamanders, earthworms, small lizards, and snakes

Eastern Coral Snake

It is very important to learn the difference between this poisonous snake and the harmless Scarlet Kingsnake that mimics it. Look for this snake's wide red and black rings with a narrow yellow ring between them. Its head is completely black. Coral Snakes like moist areas near water in pine forests, and often shelter under decaying tree trunks or leaves. They lay 3 to 12 eggs in June and the young hatch in September.

Animal group: Reptile – Family: Coral Snake
Size: 20–30 ins – Eats lizards and other (smaller) snakes
WARNING: This snake's deadly bite can kill you. Remember the "red-yellow-black" coloring means danger

Redbelly Snake

This small snake is brown, gray, or black, usually with a plain red belly. It always has three light spots at the base of its neck. The Redbelly Snake likes wooded hills or mountains and is quite widespread over the central and eastern U.S. These snakes mate in spring or fall and the female gives birth to 1 to 21 young in June to September. If alarmed, the Redbelly Snake pulls its upper lip back.

Animal group: Reptile
Family: Colubrid snake
Size: 8–16 ins
Feeds on insects,
earthworms, and slugs

Eastern Kingsnake

Animal group: Reptile – Family: Colubrid snake – Size: 36–48 ins
Eats snakes, including venomous species, small mammals,
lizards, and frogs

Also called the "Thunder snake," this shiny brown or black snake has smooth scales and a chainlike pattern of cream or white along its body. Eastern Kingsnakes live in pine and hardwood forests in the mid-Atlantic and southeastern states. They are quite secretive, and hide under logs and leaf litter. In the early morning and on warm evenings, they hunt for food, and often swim in streams to catch water snakes. Kingsnakes mate in March to June and lay clutches of 3 to 24 creamy white eggs in May to August.

Scarlet Kingsnake

This colorful snake is not poisonous, but it looks very similar to the poisonous Eastern Coral Snake. Its yellow, red, and black rings are arranged in a different pattern to the Coral Snake's rings. The Scarlet Kingsnake has yellow rings and red rings separated by black rings, but on the poisonous Coral Snake, the red and yellow bands touch. The Scarlet Kingsnake also has a red snout, not black. It is secretive, so you will not often see out in the open, except at night and after heavy rain. It prefers to hide under logs and tree bark, and is found in pine forests, tropical hardwood forests, and deciduous woodlands. Scarlet Kingsnakes mate in spring and lay 2 to 17 eggs in a rotting log in June and July, which hatch in August to September.

Animal group: Reptile
Family: Colubrid snake
Size: 14–20 ins
Eats small snakes, lizards, baby mice, small fish, insects, and earthworms

Rough Green Snake

This bright green snake lives in trees, bushes, and vines, and blends in with the background so well that you can hardly see it. Rough Green Snakes slither around by day in search of grasshoppers to eat. They are good swimmers and spend much time in and near the water. They mate in spring and fall, and lay 3 to 12 hard smooth eggs in June to August. The young hatch after 5 to 12 weeks and are greenish gray at first.

Animal group: Reptile
Family: Colubrid snake
Size: 20–30 ins
Eats grasshoppers, crickets, caterpillars, and moths

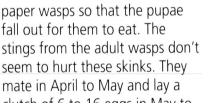

Five-lined Skink

This skink is named after the five wide, light-colored stripes on its body. As the skink grows older, these lines fade and may even disappear. In adults, the tail is usually blue to gray, and in the young it is bright blue. Breeding males have a bright orange head. Five-lined Skinks are found from New York to Florida, and west to Texas and the Great Lakes. They prefer to live on the ground, and only climb to bask in the sun. They like woodlands with logs, tree stumps, and plenty of leaf litter. Five-lined Skinks mate in spring and lay 4 to 15 eggs in a nest in May to June. The female cares for the eggs until they hatch later in the summer.

Broadhead Skink

This skink also has five light stripes on its back, but its head is broader and its body is bigger than the Five-lined Skink. Broadhead Skinks like moist woodlands with plenty of leaf litter. They often climb trees to hunt for insects to eat, and sometimes shake the nests of paper wasps so that the pupae fall out for them to eat. The stings from the adult wasps don't seem to hurt these skinks. They mate in April to May and lay a clutch of 6 to 16 eggs in May to July in a hole under a log or in leaf litter. The female guards the eggs until they hatch in June to August. This skink is often nicknamed "Scorpion", although it is completely harmless.

Animal group: Amphibian
Family: Skink
Size: 6½–12¾ ins
Feeds on insects and other small invertebrates

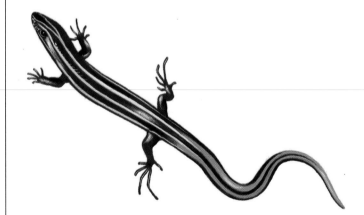

Animal group: Reptile
Family: Skink
Size: 5–8 ins
Eats insects, spiders, earthworms, lizards, crustaceans, and small mice
May also be seen in gardens and around buildings

Western Fence Lizard

This spiny lizard has a dark colored body with a pattern of matching splodges along its back. Its scales are the same size all over. Its inside legs are yellow and its belly marked with blue, hence its nickname "blue belly." Adult males also have a blue patch on the throat. The Western Fence Lizard mates in early spring, and lays 3 to 14 eggs in May to July. These lizards like mixed forests, as well as scrub and grassy areas, and you may spot them on fences, old buildings, and walls during the day.

Animal group: Reptile
Family: Iguanid
Size: 6–9 ins
Feeds on insects and other small invertebrates

Wood Turtle

The upper shell of the Wood Turtle is very rough and looks as though it has been carved. The turtle's neck and front legs are often reddish orange, which is why it is nicknamed "Redleg." Wood turtles like cool streams in deciduous woodlands. They are excellent climbers and can even climb fences. Look for a Wood Turtle after spring rains as it searches for worms to eat. The females lay one clutch of 6 to 8 eggs in May to June, which hatch in September to October.

Animal group: Reptile
Family: Pond, Marsh, and Box Turtle
Shell size: 5–9 ins
Eats slugs, insects, tadpoles, worms, and wild berries
This is a protected species in some states

Tadpole Fun

Tadpoles are the young stages of frogs, toads, newts and salamanders. The adults often live far from water, but they return in spring to mate and to lay their eggs, usually in still water. The eggs are covered in a soft jelly-like material and are called spawn.

Frogs lay their eggs in large masses which are easy to spot. Toads produce long strings of eggs and wind them around water plants. Salamanders and newts lay single eggs attached to leaves and stems. Only some of the eggs will hatch—many are eaten by predators.

Collecting spawn & tadpoles

The best place to collect spawn is from a friend's pond. Only collect from a "wild" pond if there is plenty there. Remember, it takes a great many tadpoles to produce just a few frogs because so many get eaten by fish, birds, and other predators.

1 **Collect about half a cup of spawn or a few dozen tadpoles** using a small net. Carry them home in a small bucket. Frog spawn is the easiest to find and keep.
2 **Put them into a small aquarium tank.** Use tap water that has been allowed to stand outside for a day or two to get rid of the chlorine. You can use pond water if it is not too muddy.

3 **Add a few rocks and some water plants.** Cover the tank with netting or the birds will get a free meal.
4 **Stand the tank in dappled shade.** Tadpoles like warm water, but may die if left in sunshine.
4 **Your tadpoles will need feeding a few days after they hatch.** At this stage they are vegetarian. Add small pieces of boiled lettuce leaves and 4 or 5 pellets of rabbit food every 3 or 4 days. Not too much or the water will stagnate.
5 **Change the water if it gets murky** and top up as it evaporates.

Metamorphosis

1 **Watch your tadpoles carefully and you will see them gradually change into adults.** This change is called metamorphosis (see page 4). Keep a diary of what happens. When do the red fluffy gills disappear? When do the hind and front legs first appear?

2 **If you can, record the temperature of the water in your tank on the same day once a week.** If you have two tanks, try keeping some in the cool shade and some in the warm. The warm ones should grow more quickly. Tadpoles kept really cold never change into adults, but just get bigger!

3 **When the hind legs appear** (about 5 to 6 weeks after hatching). Put some rocks in the tank for them to climb out on. They will soon need to breathe air.

4 **At this stage they need some animal food.** So give them small pieces of meat about once a week. Remove uneaten food after a couple of days or the water will get really nasty.

5 **When their front legs appear,** prop up the tank so that there is a shallow end, or build islands with small stones.

6 **The small froglets or toadlets should be released in a damp corner of your yard** or back around the edges of a pond. They are very difficult to feed at this stage and are better let go. Carry them in a box with damp moss or grass. They will drown in a bucket of water.

Streams & Rivers

Streams and rivers are a perfect place to see amphibians and reptiles that like to live near moving water, because there are always plenty of insects for them to eat in this freshwater habitat. Some prefer shallow, fast-moving streams, and others prefer slow, deep, muddy-bottomed rivers. You are most likely to find the larger salamanders and reptiles such as Spiny Softshells (turtles) in large streams and rivers.

The smaller salamanders prefer springs and streams with fewer fish to prey on them or their young. These open stretches of fresh water are often shallow at the edges, and full of rocks, pebbles, and plants which provide a place to hide or to lay eggs. Some amphibians attach their eggs to a rock in the water so that they are not washed away by the current. Salamanders like to live among rocks and leaf litter on a riverbank, and lay their eggs under a rock, or inside a rotting log, or a hole in the soil.

This picture shows five reptiles and amphibians from this book. How many do you recognize?

Spotted Frog, Tailed Frog, Pacific Giant Salamander, Western Blackneck Garter Snake, Foothill Yellow-legged Frog

Spotted Frog

The big Spotted Frog has a reddish belly and a brown back with dark spots. Its darkly masked face is embellished with a light stripe on its upper jaw. The male has extra large thumbs and is smaller than the female. These frogs live in mountainous areas in the northern Rockies and Pacific Northwest, and they like cool streams and lakes without too much plant life in the water.

Animal group: Amphibian
Family: True frog
Size: 2–4 ins
Feeds by day on small invertebrates

Canyon Treefrog

With its plump body and rough, warty skin, this frog looks more like a toad than a frog. Canyon Treefrogs are brown to olive with dark blotches. Look for them alongside rocky streams and rivers in the desert Southwest, especially in canyon bottoms. They spend most of their time on the ground, and are well disguised. They are almost the same color and pattern as the rocks where they live.

Animal group: Amphibian
Family: Treefrog
Size: 1¼–2¼ ins
Feeds at night on small invertebrates

Tailed Frog

This frog usually has a yellowish triangle on its snout and a dark stripe running from its snout across its eyes. The Tailed Frog is usually olive or brown with lots of dark spots and small warts. It lives in cool, clear, fast mountain streams on the northern Pacific coast, and in Montana and Idaho. The female attaches her eggs to rocks in the water, and the tadpoles can cling to rocks in the fast currents by sucking with their mouthparts. They take up to three years to turn into adult frogs. Tailed Frogs do not have proper tails, as their name suggests, but the males have a tail-like organ for fertilizing eggs.

Animal group: Amphibian
Family: Tailed frog
Size: 1–2 ins
Tadpoles feed on algae and small invertebrates in the water, while adults feed on insects and other invertebrates

Foothill Yellow-legged Frog

This frog is named after the yellow coloring on the underside of its legs. Its skin is gray or olive, and its back is sometimes mottled with gray. Yellow-legged Frogs live in western Oregon to southern California, and like gravelly or sandy streams with sunny banks and woodlands close by. If alarmed, they dive into the water and hide among the rocks at the bottom of the stream until danger has passed. They mate in spring, and the females usually attach their eggs to rocks under water.

Animal group: Amphibian
Family: True frog
Size: 1¾–3 ins
Feeds on invertebrates

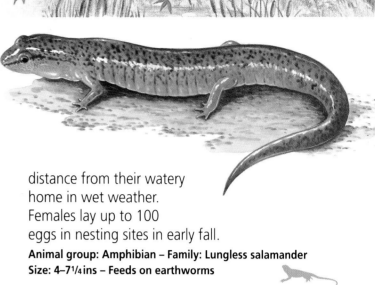

Northern Red Salamander

This plump Northern Red Salamander is one of the easiest eastern salamanders to recognize, with its yellow eyes and bright red body covered with black dots. The young are usually coral-red or orange, and they become darker as they grow older. Adults can be orange-brown to purplish. These salamanders like cool, clear water, and you can find them in and around brooks, streams, and springs. See if you can spot a Red Salamander searching for food in leaf litter. They often wander quite a distance from their watery home in wet weather. Females lay up to 100 eggs in nesting sites in early fall.

Animal group: Amphibian – Family: Lungless salamander
Size: 4–7¹/₄ ins – Feeds on earthworms

Pacific Giant Salamander

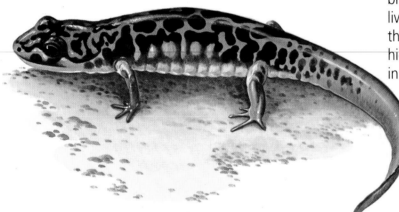

This big, smooth-skinned salamander is purplish or brown, mottled with black. Its belly is usually light brown to yellowish white. Adult Giant Salamanders live in or around rivers and streams that flow through cool woodlands in the Pacific Northwest, hiding under rocks, leaf litter and logs. They breed in spring and lay their eggs in water. The young live in water, where they eat insects and the tadpoles of Tailed Frogs. They sometimes eat each other, too.

Animal group: Amphibian
Family: Mole salamander – Size: 7–11³/₄ ins
Adults feed on other salamanders, garter snakes, large insects and mice.

Spring Salamander

The Spring Salamander is named after the cool springs in the Appalachians where it lives, but you can also see it in mountain streams, or hiding under rotting logs nearby. It is one of the largest lungless salamanders, and is pinkish orange, patterned with darker markings. These salamanders breed during the warm summer months and lay up to 100 eggs one at a time, attached to stones in the water.

Animal group: Amphibian
Family: Lungless salamander – Size: 4¹/₄–8³/₄ ins

Sometimes hunts on land on wet nights for insects and small salamanders, but little is known of its habits
Also found in wet caves

Southern Two-lined Salamander

Can you guess where this salamander gets its name? Two dark lines run from its eye all the way to the tip of its tail, so it is easy to spot. You may see one of these salamanders near a rocky brook or stream in eastern areas, but they are quite shy and dash away to hide under leaf litter or a rock if alarmed. Two-lined Salamanders lay up to a hundred eggs in the water under rocks, logs, or plants. Sometimes the female guards the eggs until they hatch.

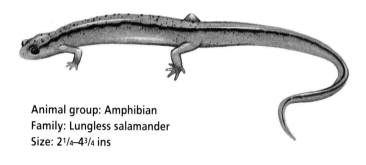

Animal group: Amphibian
Family: Lungless salamander
Size: 2¹/₄–4³/₄ ins

This pretty salamander is often yellow to orange-red with black spots on its body and a herringbone pattern on its tail. The slim tail is very long indeed, which makes it easy to tell this salamander apart from others. Longtail Salamanders live in streams and springs in woodland areas. They breed in the fall to spring, then lay eggs in underground holes close to the stream where they live. They often come out on warm rainy nights to search for food on the woodland floor.

Longtail Salamander

Animal group: Amphibian
Family: Lungless salamander – Size: 7–8 ins
Feeds on tiny insects and other invertebrates

Dusky Salamander

The Dusky Salamander lives in rocky woodland streams and creeks in much of the East. The adults come in many colours and patterns, but are usually tan or brown. The young have five to eight pairs of yellowish spots on their backs. The tail is triangular in cross-section. Dusky salamanders breed in summer and lay up to three dozen eggs under rocks, in rotting logs, and in holes in the bank of a stream.

Animal group: Amphibian
Family: Lungless salamander – Size: 2¹/₂–5¹/₂ ins
Feeds on insect larvae, sow bugs, and earthworms

Western Blackneck Garter Snake

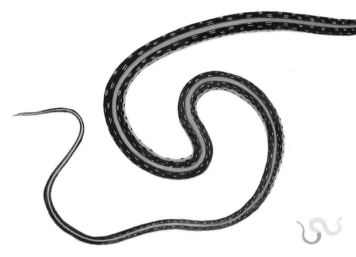

The Blackneck Garter Snake is olive-gray or brown with a yellow stripe down the middle of its back and two large black splodges on its neck. It lives in canyon and mountain streams and springs in the southwest, and swims along searching for prey. This snake is active during the day, and you may see one soaking up the sun on a rock. These snakes give birth to 7 to 25 young in summer.

Animal group: Amphibian – Family: Colubrid snake
Size: 16–43 ins – Feeds on toads, frogs and tadpoles

Greater Siren

With its long, thick, gray-green body and tiny legs, you could easily think this, the largest salamander in North America, is an eel. The Greater Siren lives in shallow, muddy streams filled with weeds, and, like the Mudpuppy, keeps the gilled, larval form all its life. During the day, it lies buried in mud under rocks or water plants. If the stream where it lives dries up in summer, the Siren keeps moist by spreading slime from its skin all over its body, like a cocoon. Sirens can live for up to twenty-five years.

Animal group: Amphibian
Family: Siren
Size: 20–38 ins
Feeds at night on snails, small fish, water plants, and insect larvae

Mud Puppy

This large water-dwelling salamander lives in rivers and streams in much of central North America, including muddy waters that are overgrown with weeds. It is gray to brown with dark blue spots, and its belly is gray with dark spots. A Mud Puppy never turns into a land-dwelling, air-breathing adult, but looks like a larva all its life, with feathery gills on its head. Mud Puppies breed in summer, and the female lays up to 190 eggs attached to a stone or log under water, which she guards until they hatch.

Animal group: Amphibian
Family: Mud Puppy and Waterdog – Size: 8–17 ins
Feeds at night on worms, crayfish, insects, and small fish

Spiny Softshell

Instead of a hard, horny shell, this turtle has a soft, one made of thick, brown skin marked with round spots with a line around the edge. Apart from that, this turtle's long neck and tubelike snout help you to tell it apart from other turtles. Spiny Softshells can live just as well in boggy ponds as in rivers and lakes. They like to sunbathe, but they can move quickly both on land and in water, so you will be lucky to see one up close.

Animal group: Reptile
Family: Softshell turtle
Shell size: 5–9¼ ins (male), 6–18 ins (female)
Feeds on minnows and other water creatures
WARNING: This turtle can give a painful bite

Hellbender

This huge, slimy salamander is brown or gray, looks flattened around the head and body and a flapping curtain of skin along its length. The Hellbender spends its whole life in water, and particularly likes rushing rivers with lots of nice flat stones on the river bed to hide under. The male is smaller than the female, and in the breeding season he makes a nest under a big flat rock or log. The female lays up to 500 eggs, and the male often guards them until the larvae hatch two or three months later. Hellbenders are also called "Devil Dogs," but despite their fearsome names, they are completely harmless.

Animal group: Amphibian
Family: Giant salamander – Size: 12–29 ins
Feeds on snails, crayfish, and worms

Focus on snakes

People who have never handled a snake often think its skin will feel cold and slimy. In fact snakes have dry scaly waterproof skins. Unlike you, snakes never stop growing and soon become too big for their skins. Young snakes shed their skins about seven times in their first year when they are growing fast. Adults change skins 2–3 times a year.

Snakebite prevention

Snakes bite to subdue their prey so that they can kill and eat it. Some will also bite in self-defense if frightened, stepped on or picked up. Given a chance, a snake will run away from you just as fast as you run away from it!

- **Wear boots or stout shoes and thick trousers** in snake territory. Avoid wearing sneakers.
- **Look and take care where you put your hands and feet.**
- **Carry a light when walking outside at night.**
- **Learn to recognize the poisonous species** and where they are found. Rattlesnakes, coral snakes, cottonmouths, and copperheads are all poisonous.

First Aid

- **If bitten, remain calm.** Snakebite, even from poisonous species, is rarely fatal. The snake may only inject a small amount of venom.
- **Lie down on one side and send someone for help. Or walk slowly toward help.** This will help to stop the spread of the venom in the blood. Keep as still as possible until you reach the doctor or hospital.
- **Try to remember what the snake looked like.** This will help the doctor to know which anti-venom to give you.
- **If you have learnt First Aid** and cannot get to hospital within 30 minutes or so:
  1 Bandage the whole limb as for a sprain, starting at the fingers or toes.
  2 Immobilize the limb with a sling for an arm or splints for a leg, if necessary.

Making cards

A shed snake skin may look delicate but is actually quite tough. You can make interesting greeting cards, book marks and pictures from it.

1 **Fold a piece of art paper to make a blank card.** Draw your favorite snake on it and color in using bright colors.

New skin for old

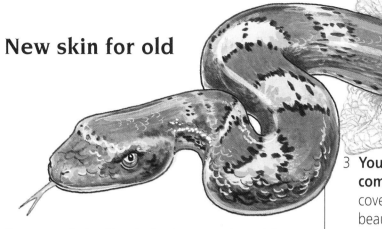

If you can find a friend who keeps snakes, visit a zoo or vivarium, you may be able to watch a snake shedding its skin.

1 **A few days before it sheds its skin**, the snake's eyes will go cloudy and its skin looks dull.

2 **The skin splits first along the lips.** The snake rubs its head along the ground to roll the skin back. Then it gradually crawls free as the skin turns inside out. It's rather like turning your sock inside out as you pull your leg out.

3 **You will be left with a ghostly snake skin complete with every scale** and even the covering of the eyes. The snake's new skin is beautifully clean and bright.

4 **Ask if you can keep the skin.** Look out for shed snake skins in areas where you know snakes live. Stick them in your field note book and note the date and place where you found them.

5 **Look at the underside of the skin.** Notice that the belly scales are much larger than the others. By counting these scales and looking at the head pattern, experienced naturalists can tell which species shed the skin.

6 **You can make a dragon in a similar way.** Use the large belly scales for the pointed scales on the dragon's back. Draw in ears, tail, flames and any other missing pieces afterwards. Stick on a plastic eye or draw one in.

2 **Lightly spread paper glue inside the snake's outline.** Be careful not to glue outside the lines.

3 **Stick pieces of snake skin over the snake** and trim off the edges outside the snake's outline.

4 **Color in the background** if you want to.

5 **Cover the card with sticky plastic film** for protection.

Lakes, Ponds & Marshes

A still, freshwater lake or pond is an ideal place to watch reptiles and amphibians that live in and around the water. During the breeding season, from late winter to early spring, this habitat rings with the mating calls of frogs as they sit on water plants and sing in chorus. For many people, the first sign of spring is the shrill call of the Spring Peeper. Some reptiles and amphibians may live on the shore of a lake while others live in the trees overhanging the water.

Ponds and lakes are also important to some reptiles and amphibians that spend the rest of the year in a different habitat, such as a nearby woodland. Spotted Salamanders migrate each year to breeding pools to lay their eggs, then return at once to their other home in the woods.

Many amphibians breed in the temporary pools brought by spring rain or melted snow, even though these pools contain no fish or other food to eat. Other wetland habitats such as marshes and the edges of ponds and lakes are among the most threatened habitats in North America. Millions of acres of marsh, swamp, and bog have been drained, and many species of reptile and amphibian living there are now endangered.

This picture shows five reptiles and amphibians from this book. How many do you recognize?

Spotted Turtle, Mud Turtle, Western Ribbon Snake, Green Frog, Gray Treefrog

Common Gray Treefrog

Gray Treefrogs usually spend the day up in the branches of high trees growing beside lakes in the eastern U.S., but they come down at night. Listen for their loud, trilling call during the breeding season in spring and early summer. These frogs have rough gray to greenish gray coloring, with large dark blotches, which helps to disguise them against the bark of their treetop home. They have a pale spot rimmed with black below each eye, and their inner thighs are bright yellow or orange.

Animal group: Amphibian
Family: Treefrog
Size: 1¼–2½ ins – Eats insects

Green Treefrog

This brilliant green frog has a pale stripe running from its upper jaw down the side of its body. It is not always green and may be yellow or greenish gray. Occasionally it has tiny gold dots on its back. You can often find one of these frogs dozing under a large leaf or in other damp, shady places during the day. Green Treefrogs gather together in huge groups to sing, and the males call while clinging on to the stems of water plants. In the distance, their song sounds like a cow bell. These frogs always like to walk rather than jump.

Animal group: Amphibian
Family: Treefrog
Size: 1¼–2½ ins
Eats insects and other small invertebrates

Northern Cricket Frog

You are quite likely to see one of these rough-skinned frogs hopping around during the day. They have a black triangular mark on their foreheads and their color can be black, brown, green, yellow or red. Cricket Frogs can hop quite quickly even though their legs are short. They like shallow ponds with plenty of plant life, and sunny, slow-moving streams, where they can sunbathe on the edge. Cricket Frogs are so named because their song sounds like the call of a cricket.

Animal group: Amphibian
Family: Treefrog
Size: 1/2–1 1/2 ins
Eats insects and other small invertebrates

Spring Peeper

Although hearing a chorus of these frogs is said to signal the beginning of spring, they sound more like Santa's jingle bells. Listen for them calling to each other from dead grass and the base of shrubs in woodland and meadow ponds in the eastern U.S. Spring Peepers can be dark or light brown or gray, and they have a big cross marked on their backs. They live in wet woodlands and are out and about at night. In winter, they hibernate under logs and loose bark.

Animal group: Amphibian
Family: Treefrog
Size: 3/4–1 1/2 ins
Eats insects and small invertebrates

Upland Chorus Frog

These frogs love to sing and can be heard in many parts of the eastern and southern U.S.; they make a scraping, grating sound . Although you may hear them you will be lucky to see one as they are shy and hop into the water at the slightest movement. Chorus Frogs live in most grassy areas near lakes, ponds, swamps, and rivers. They are brown, gray or green, with smooth skin and thin black lines. They also have a black line running across the eye and a white line on their top jaw.

Animal group: Amphibian
Family: Treefrog – Size: 3/4–1 1/2 ins
Eats insects and small invertebrates

Lakes, Ponds & Marshes

Red-legged Frog

During the day, you can see this big frog searching for food around ponds and lakes along the West Coast. It is named after the red on the underside of its hind legs. Its back is reddish brown to gray, with darker blotches and specks. Its belly is mainly yellow and fades into red. There is usually a dark mask pattern on its face and a white line on its jaw. These frogs breed in January to March and lay masses of eggs in the water.

Animal group: Amphibian
Family: True frog – Size: 2–8 ins
Eats insects and other
small invertebrates
Also found
in damp
woodlands

Pickerel Frog

This frog is smooth-skinned, with two rows of dark square spots along its back. Its belly and the underside of its hind legs are a clear yellowy orange. It has a light stripe on its jaw. You can find it in all the eastern U.S. apart from the far southeast. It likes to be near swamps and slow-moving streams. Its call is a low croak. Sometimes it croaks underwater and sounds as though it is snoring. It wards off enemies by releasing a stinging fluid from its skin.

Animal group: Amphibian
Family: True frog
Size: 1³/₄–3¹/₂ ins
Eats insects and other
small invertebrates

This frog has two raised ridges down each side of its back. A Green Frog may be greenish brown or bronze with brown blotches. Its belly is white with a pattern of lines or spots, and the males have a yellow throat. You can see Green Frogs in many parts of eastern North America. They like shallow ponds, lakesides, swamps, and marshes.

Animal group: Amphibian
Family: True frog
Size: 2¹/₄–4 ins
Hunts at night for insects and
other small invertebrates

Green Frog

Animal group: Amphibian
Family: True toad
Size: 2½–5 ins
Eats insects and other small invertebrates

Western Toad

This big, warty toad is grayish green, with a cream stripe down the center of its back. Its reddish warts are surrounded by black blotches. Western Toads like damp areas in woodlands, alpine meadows, arid scrub, and low grasslands, from the central Rockies to California and southern Alaska. They live in a burrow which they make themselves, or in the burrow of another animal such as a mouse. Listen for their call, a sound like the "peep-peep" of baby chicks.

Bullfrog

Listen for the bullfrog's call in the morning; it sounds like "jug o'rum"and will carry for a long way on a still day. By reaching a size of 8 inches the Bullfrog can make a valid claim to be the biggest frog in North America. Its body varies in color from yellow to green and is usually marked with gray. Its belly is whitish, and might have gray splodges too. It has large visible eardrums behind each eye, often even bigger than its eyes. Bullfrogs like spacious stretches of water to move around in with enough foliage to give good cover. They are active at night when you might see them on the banks of lakes and ponds. If they are alarmed, they hop into the undergrowth or into the water. Bullfrog tadpoles may take up to two years to turn into adults.

Animal group: Amphibian
Family: True frog
Size: 3½–8 ins
Eats other frogs, insects, crayfish, and sometimes eats small birds and snakes too

Lakes, Ponds & Marshes

Northern Water Snake

You can see this snake in many parts of eastern North America around lakes, ponds, rivers, ditches, and bogs. It is usually out and about day and night searching for food. It also likes to bask in the sun. The Northern Water Snake is brownish or gray with darker splodges on its back and sides, and dark bands in the neck area. Its belly is light, and often marked with a jumble of reddish half-moon shapes. They mate in late spring, and give birth to up to thirty young in late summer to early fall. This snake is not venomous, but it is easily confused with the Cottonmouth (see page 52), which has a deadly bite.

Animal group: Reptile
Family: Colubrid snake
Size: 22–53 ins
Eats salamanders, turtles,
frogs, and small fish

Red-spotted Eastern Newt

This is the adult of the colorful Red Eft on page 19. The adults live in water, whereas the efts live on land. Red-spotted Newts are yellowish brown or olive-green, with red spots on their back, edged with black. They live in and around ponds, small lakes, marshes, and streams. These newts breed from late winter to early spring, and lay up to 400 eggs, one at a time, on water plants.

Animal group: Amphibian
Family: Salamandrid – Size: 2$\frac{1}{2}$–5 ins
Eats worms, crustaceans, insects, and mollusks

Diamondback Water Snake

This snake is named after the dark brown, chainlike pattern on its lighter brown back. It is active by day, and you may spot one basking on a log on the edge of a lake, pond, river, stream, swamp, or ditch. Diamondback Water Snakes mate in spring and lay up to sixty-two young in August to October. These snakes are not venomous, but are aggressive and quick to bite. They can be also confused with the Cottonmouth (see page 52).

Animal group: Reptile
Family: Colubrid snake
Size: 30–63 ins
Eats fish and frogs

American Alligator

The alligator's tough, knobbly skin is mostly dark, with lighter bands going around its body. Commonly reaching 8 to 10 feet, it is North America's biggest reptile. It has a wide snout and when its mouth is closed you can't see its teeth (unlike the very rare American Crocodile which can't hide its teeth at all). Alligators live in the lakes, swamps, bayous, ponds, and marshes of the southeast coast from North Carolina to Texas, and several hundred miles inland. They hibernate in winter, then come out of their den in spring to breed. You can hear males bellowing to each other from a long way off. The female lays her eggs in a nest of mud and leaves, and stays close until the young hatch about nine weeks later. American Alligators look after their young for 1 to 6 years. Once an endangered species, the alligator is now common in many areas.

Animal group: Reptile – Family: Crocodile – Size: 6–19¼ feet
Eats fish, crustaceans, insects (when young),
as well as birds, snakes, frogs and small mammals

Red-eared Slider

This pretty turtle is easy to recognize because, as its name suggests, it has red marks behind each eye, like little red ears. Red-eared Sliders enjoy basking in the sun, and you can often see a crowd of them piled on top of each other on a favorite log. They live in ponds, lakes, swamps, slow rivers, and shallow streams in the Mississippi drainage and southern Plains. They mate in March to June and lay one to three clutches of up to twenty-three eggs in a hole in the ground. These turtles are also called "Pond Sliders."

Animal group: Reptile
Family: Pond and Box Turtle – Shell size: 5–11½ ins
The young eat tadpoles, water insects, crustaceans, and
mollusks. They start eating plants as they grow older

Lakes, Ponds & Marshes

Spotted Turtle

This little Spotted Turtle is one of the prettiest turtles, and one of the easiest to recognize. Its shell is black patterned with yellow dots. Females have orange eyes and a yellow chin, and males have brown eyes, a tan chin, and a long, thick tail. Spotted Turtles mate in early spring, and in early summer the female lays up to eight eggs in a shallow nest that she digs in a sunny place. Look for these turtles in early spring sitting on logs at the edge of ponds and shallow-bottomed streams along the East Coast.

Animal group: Reptile   Family: Pond, Marsh, and Box Turtle
Shell size: 3¹/₂–5 ins   Eats insects and water plants

Common Musk Turtle

Also known as "Stinkpot" and "Stinking Jim" because it produces a nasty-smelling fluid from glands in its skin when it is disturbed. They have two pale lines on its head and a green, brown or dark gray shell, often looking green with algae. It lives in shallow waters in many parts of eastern North America. You may spot one in spring sunbathing in the water with the top of its shell in the sun. They can climb trees to reach the sun. Musk Turtles mate under water and lay 3 to 5 eggs in a shallow nest on the pond bank or beneath rotting logs. The males are quick to bite.

Animal group: Reptile – Family: Musk and Mud Turtle
Shell size: 3–5¹/₂ ins – Eats snails, clams, and other invertebrates as well as aquatic plants

This turtle lives in overgrown swamps and ponds, especially along southeast coastal areas and the lower Mississippi basin. As its name suggests, the Mud Turtle spends most of its time on the muddy bottom. If the water in the pond or swamp dries up, the turtle can burrow into the mud and survive there until it rains and the water returns. A Mud Turtle's shell is olive to dark brown and smooth on top, and yellow to brown below. Males have a blunt spine at the end of the tail. During the summer, these turtles spend more time on land. They breed in spring, and the female lays one to six eggs in a hole that she digs in the soil. These turtles sometimes lay their eggs in muskrat or beaver lodges.

Mud Turtle

Animal group: Reptile
Family: Musk and Mud Turtle
Shell size: 3–5 ins
Eats a variety of invertebrates and aquatic plants

Western Painted Turtle

Painted Turtles are the most widespread turtles in North America, and the Western Painted Turtle is the biggest. The top of its smooth, oval shell is olive or black with red bars, and slightly flattened. The underside is yellow, and there are yellow stripes on its neck, legs, and tail. These turtles live in sluggish water in shallow streams, lakes, and rivers, and they like to sunbathe on logs in large groups. These turtles nest in early summer and lay one or two clutches of eggs in northern areas, and two to four clutches in the South.

Animal group: Reptile
Family: Pond, Marsh, and Box Turtle
Shell size: 4–10 ins
Eats small fish, tadpoles, frogs, and water plants

Snapping Turtle

The huge head, strong jaws, and very long, toothed-edged tail will help you to spot this turtle. It has a vicious bite, so keep well clear. Snapping Turtles like to be in warm, shallow, muddy water with lots of plant life, and often bury themselves up to their eyes in mud. They mate in spring, and lay up to 80 eggs in a hole in the ground a few weeks later. They eat birds, fish, plants, in fact anything that presents itself as available food. Snapping Turtles are very good swimmers.

Animal group: Reptile
Family: Snapping Turtle
Shell size: 8–18½ ins
Eats fish, birds, small mammals, water plants, invertebrates, and even dead animals

Western Ribbon Snake

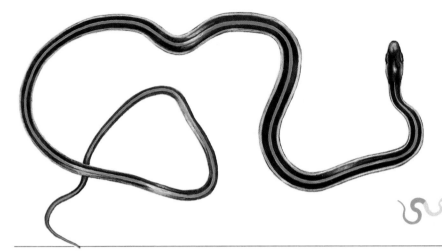

Slim and ribbon-like, this garter snake slithers among the weeds at the water's edge, searching for food. It is dark in color with three light stripes running along its body. After mating in the spring, as many as 25 young may be born in mid to late summer. Many are eaten by predators.

Animal group: Reptile
Family: Colubrid snake
Size: 19–48$\frac{1}{2}$ ins
Eats small fish, frogs and tadpoles

Cottonmouth

The Cottonmouth is so called because of its hostile habit of opening its mouth to reveal the "white cotton" lining. It does this to "spook" or scare aware predators and unwelcome visitors. It is a water snake and the only one to swim with its head above the water. A heavy looking, dark colored snake, it has a wide, flat top to its head and may have a brown stripe on each side of its face. It is very dangerous with a bite that can kill you! Cottonmouths give birth to up to 15 young in late summer, after mating in the spring. You can spot the young cottonmouth easily because of their yellow tails. They like to live in many different water habitats from ditches to mountain streams.

Animal group: Reptile – Family: Pit viper – Size: 20–74 ins
Hunts at night for frogs, fish, snakes, and birds
WARNING: Avoid. This snake's bite is very poisonous and can kill you

Wandering Garter Snake

You may be lucky enough to see this snake sunbathing in the morning at the edge of ponds, lakes, and streams from New Mexico to British Colombia and Nevada. It has an indistinct yellowish brown stripe along its back. Wandering Garter Snakes go out hunting during the day. They mate in spring and give birth to 4 to 19 young in July to September.

Animal group: Reptile
Family: Colubrid snake
Size: 18–42 ins
Eats frogs, slugs, tadpoles, fish, worms, and small birds
Also found in damp meadows, open grassland and forest near water

Queen Snake

A strong swimmer, the Queen Snake is active both day and night. It is olive brown to dark brown, with a yellowish stripe along the sides of its body and four brown stripes on its yellow belly. Queen Snakes are found in many water habitats, including the edges of cool lakes, fast-flowing streams, small, rocky rivers, and sandy-bottomed creeks. They mate in April to May, and females give birth to 5 to 23 young in late summer. You may spot one of these snakes sunbathing on a tree branch overhanging the water. But if it notices you, it will drop into the water below and disappear in a flash.

Animal group: Reptile
Family: Colubrid snake
Size: 16–36³/₄ ins
Eats mainly crayfish

Massasauga Rattlesnake

You'll find this snake in swamps around estuaries and that's where it got its name: "massasauga" is "river mouth" in Chippewa. They are also found in bogs, marshland, flood plains, and grassy wetlands. The Massasauga rattlesnake differs from other rattlesnakes by having nine large scales on the top of its head. Its body has dark splodges in a regular pattern and it has a dark strip going from its eye to the back of its neck. They mate from April to May, and give birth to 2 to 19 young in July to September. You may see one of these snakes basking in the sun on mild days.

Animal group: Reptile
Family: Pit viper
Size: 18–39¹/₂ ins
Eats frogs, lizards, and small rodents
WARNING: While not as venomous as some rattlesnakes, the Massasauga can deliver a dangerous bite if provoked.
Do not approach

Keeping Lizards

Lizards can make fascinating pets. You will learn a lot from watching them and caring for them. Given the right living conditions, they will live happily for many years and be lots of fun. They make better pets than turtles which usually die in captivity before they reach adulthood.

However, before you begin, THINK! Are you willing to spend time and money looking after your pet? A lizard or any other pet cannot be released or thrown away if you get bored of it. Read and learn as much as you can about your chosen animal BEFORE you buy it.

Equipment

This list tells you some of the things you will need to keep a lizard. You should also take advice from a vet and pet stores.

Try to make your lizard's home as near to its natural habitat as possible. But also make sure you can observe your pet easily. You will need:

1 **A glass or plastic aquarium at least 30 inches long and 12 inches wide.** Buy a bigger one if you can. Secondhand will do as it doesn't have to be waterproof. Later, if your pet succeeds in charming your family, you may be able to build a larger vivarium!

2 **A sturdy lid to prevent escapes and to support lights (see below).** Strong wire mesh may do but it must be firmly held down. It should be hinged or easy to remove.

3 **Your lizard will need two kinds of light.** An ultra-violet (UV) light for health, (buy one made specially for reptiles) and a basking light for warmth.

4 **A thermometer and possibly a heater.**

5 **Places to hide and climb** like an opaque plastic box with a hole in one side; bamboo sections; drift wood or slabs of bark.

6 **Cover the floor of the tank with 1–2 inches of fine sand or smooth gravel.** Or you can use pine bark mulch or shredded bark and soil (called orchid bark mix). Get it from your pet store.

Choosing your lizard

Wild lizards are best left free. They have families and homes. You will have more fun watching them than catching them. They may also have parasites and be difficult to tame.

1 **Go to a reputable dealer and ask for captive-bred lizards.** These have not been taken from the wild and are used to captivity. Find out as much as possible about your chosen species before buying it.
2 **For your first lizard, choose a relatively cheap, hardy lizard.** Find out which species are easiest to keep. A healthy, lively, small brown lizard is more interesting than a brightly-colored, exotic species that dies after a few weeks.
3 **There are many American species that make good pets.** If you choose a "foreigner" make sure you can provide it with the right conditions.
4 **You only need one.** Lizards are territorial and will fight each other in a confined space.
4 **Make sure that the animal you buy has been well looked afte**r in the store. Otherwise it may soon die from shock and stress.
5 **Check whether you need a permit to keep your pet.**

Gecko guests

If you are lucky, you may have a gecko visit you. Several species commonly share our houses especially in Florida and along the Gulf Coast. Geckos should be made welcome. They do no harm and are expert bug catchers! Mosquitoes, flies, and moths will disappear while you sleep! Watch them:
• **Run up walls and along ceilings**. They do this using special pads on their fingers and toes. The pads are made up of overlapping flaps covered in microscopic (tiny), backward-pointing bristles. These are so small they can grip onto the tiniest irregularity. There may also be minute suction cups on the ends of the bristles.
If you can find a gecko climbing up glass, you will be able to look at the underneath of its feet.

• **Lick their eyes**: they do this to clean their eyes which have no eyelids.
• **Change their skin**: lizard skin flakes off in large pieces.
• **Catch a fly**: they have huge eyes to help them to see in the dark.

Prairies & Grasslands

Grasslands stretch across the middle of North America, from the Midwest south to Texas, west to the Rockies, and north into Canada. They are large areas of long or short grass where crops grow and animals graze. They include the Great Plains, the prairies, and some meadow areas in the East and West.

Ground-dwelling reptiles and amphibians that can survive hot dry summers live in this habitat. Many of them find protection from predators and the sun by living underground. There are hardly any trees there, but the grass provides shelter. Some animals, such as the Green Grass Snake are so well camouflaged that they are almost invisible.

This picture shows five reptiles and amphibians from this book. How many do you recognize?

Western Skink, Long-toed Salamander, Prairie Rattlesnake, Smooth Green Snake, Six-lined Racerunner

Long-toed Salamander

This slender salamander lives in grassland areas under logs, tree bark, or rocks, close to lakes and streams. It is dark brown to black on top, with a light, blotchy stripe along its back, and, as its name suggests, it has long toes. It breeds in ponds and rain pools from as early as January in the South to July in the North. The female often lays the eggs one at a time near the surface. The young are only about ½ inch long when they hatch, and turn into adults when they are 2–4 inches long.

Animal group: Amphibian
Family: Iguanid – Size: 2½–4½ ins
Feeds on insects and small invertebrates
Also found in moist evergreen forests and alpine meadows

Western Chorus Frog

You can hear this frog croaking on warm spring evenings in many parts of the upper Midwest and Plains. The males sit on floating plant leaves and call to the females, making a noise that sounds like someone running their finger across a pocket comb. In warm areas these frogs breed in very early spring, but in the cooler North they wait until midsummer. Chorus Frogs are smooth-skinned, and are usually greenish gray or brown with three dark stripes down the back.

Animal group: Amphibian – Family: Treefrog – Size: ¾–1½ ins
Hunts at night for small invertebrates
Also found in woodlands, swamps, farmland

Plains Spadefoot

This chubby, grey-brown toad has a bump between its eyes and a black wedge-shaped spade on each hind foot. You can find these toads in fields and shortgrass prairies in the Great Plains and eastern Rockies. They like sandy soil. Listen for their call, which sounds like a quacking duck. They breed in summer when it rains. The female lays a mass of eggs in a shallow pool or puddle, attached to plant stems. The eggs hatch into tadpoles within forty-eight hours. The tadpoles usually eat algae, but may become carnivorous and eat each other. Those that survive grow into adults within two months.

Animal group: Amphibian
Family: Spadefoot toad
Size: 1½–2½ ins
Hunts at night for insects and other invertebrates

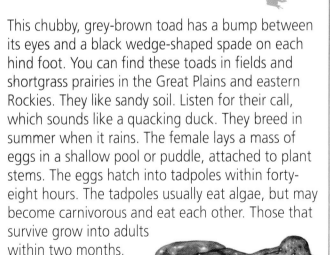

Great Plains Toad

This large toad is gray to olive-brown and covered in dark blotches with light edges. It is active mainly at night but you may see it searching for food by day in rainy weather. These toads are popular with farmers because their favorite food is cutworms, which eat farm crops. If threatened, it puffs out its body, closes its eyes, and puts its head close to the ground, looking more like a stone than a toad. Great Plains Toads breed during or after heavy rain, then the female lays a string of eggs at the bottom of a rain puddle.

Animal group: Amphibian
Family: True toad
Size: 2–4½ ins
Eats insects and other small invertebrates, particularly cutworms

Collared Lizard

One of the most striking of all lizards is this Collared Lizard, with its black and white collar and colorful yellow, brown, or green-blue body. The mature male has a yellow or orange throat (sometimes blue in the West). This lizard can be quite bad-tempered and will bite if provoked. When escaping from a predator, it lifts up its tail and rushes along on its hind legs like a tiny dinosaur. Look for one on rocky and sandy plains jumping from rock to rock as it chases after prey. These lizards also like to bask in the sun on boulders. They breed from April to June and lay 1 to 12 eggs in midsummer.

Animal group: Reptile
Family: Iguanid
Size: 8–14 ins
Feeds on insects and other lizards
Also found in forested areas

Lesser Earless Lizard

This small lizard usually has rows of dark blotches along the center of its back. The male has two black bars behind its armpit and the female has an orange throat in the breeding season. The Lesser Earless Lizard has long legs and toes, and no external ears, which is why it can burrow headfirst into the sand so speedily to hide. These lizards live on sandy prairies and are active during the day. When the sun is at its hottest, they stay in the shade or in the burrow of another animal. They breed in spring and summer and lay 5 to 7 eggs.

Animal group: Reptile – Family: Iguanid
Size: 4–5¼ ins – Feeds on small spiders and insects

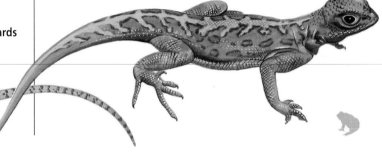

The only whiptail lizard in the eastern U.S., the yellow and brown Racerunner has six or seven light stripes. It looks like a skink, but its skin is not as shiny. Males have a green or blue throat, and females have a white throat. Racerunners are well named because they can usually outrun a predator, and they are also nicknamed "Field Streaks" because of their speed. These lizards are most active on warm mornings, when you can see them hunting or basking in the sun. At night and in cool weather, they burrow in the sand. Look for them in dry, sunny grasslands from the mid-Atlantic coast west to the central and southern Great Plains. They mate in spring and early summer, and lay two clutches of eggs.

Six-lined Racerunner

Animal group: Reptile
Family: Whiptail lizard
Size: 6–10½ ins
Feeds on insects and other small invertebrates
Also found in open woodlands

Short-horned Lizard

The Short-horned Lizard is quite easy to recognize by the crown of short spines on its head. You can tell this lizard apart from the Desert Horned Lizard because it has one row of spines along its body instead of two. It lives on rocky and sandy plains, and you are most likely to see it during the warmest part of the day. After dark it digs a burrow to sleep in. The female gives birth to 6 to 31 young in summer. These lizards are quite hardy, and can survive cooler temperatures than the other species of horned lizards.

Animal group:

Reptile
Family: Iguanid
Size: 2½–5 ins
Eats mostly ants and other insects and invertebrates

Western Skink

This skink has a brown stripe down its back from head to tail, with a light stripe on either side of the brown. During the mating season, the male has orange patches on the sides of his head and on the tip of his tail. The Western Skink lives in rocky grassland areas and is active by day but tends to hide under stones, dead leaves and logs. The female lays a clutch of 2 to 6 eggs in summer, which she cares for until they hatch. The young have bright blue tails.

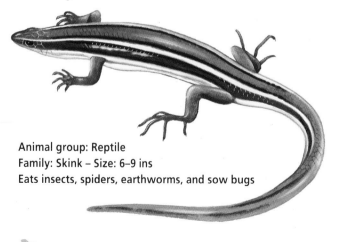

Animal group: Reptile
Family: Skink – Size: 6–9 ins
Eats insects, spiders, earthworms, and sow bugs

Great Plains Skink

This is the largest skink in the U.S., and it lives on the rocky grasslands of the Great Plains and southwest. It has smooth scales and is sometimes patterned with indistinct stripes. The young are jet black with orange and white spots on the head and a bright blue tail. These skinks are secretive, so you will be lucky to see one. They hide under rocks and can give a very painful bite if they are disturbed. They mate in spring, and lay 7 to 21 eggs in a nest under a rock. The female cares for the eggs until they hatch in summer.

Animal group: Reptile
Family: Skink
Size: 6½–13¾ ins
Feeds on insects, spiders, and small lizards
WARNING: This skink can give a painful bite

Western Coachwhip

This large, long-tailed snake is possibly the fastest snake in the U.S. It is usually pinkish, olive, yellowish, or light brown above, with very little patterning. It slithers around during the day searching for food. If this snake is chased, it may climb a tree or dart into a mammal's burrow. If cornered, it coils itself up, vibrates its tail, and strikes at the attacker. Western Coachwhips like dry, open grasslands. They mate in spring, laying clutches of 4 to 16 eggs in summer.

Animal group: Reptile
Family: Colubrid snake – Size: 36–102 ins
Eats other snakes, lizards, grasshoppers, birds, and small rodents

Striped Whipsnake

Animal group: Reptile
Family: Colubrid snake
Size: 40–72 ins
Eats lizards, birds, small mammals, and snakes
Also found in open pine and oak woodlands and rugged mountainous areas

This long, slim snake is alert and fast-moving, and if surprised, it will speed into a mammal burrow or under rocks to hide. It usually has two or more white or cream stripes along each side of its body, which make it easier to spot. The Striped Whipsnake hunts by day. It will climb trees in search of young birds to eat or to find a place to sunbathe. Striped Whipsnakes mate in spring and may make a nest in an old mammal burrow. The female lays 3 to 12 eggs in summer.

Checkered Garter Snake

Patterned like a chessboard, this snake likes dry grassland areas close to flowing water. It is active by day, when it hunts for food. These snakes give birth to 6 to 18 young in summer. You are most likely to see one in the southwest and Texas.

Animal group: Reptile
Family: Colubrid snake – Size: 18–42½ ins
Eats frogs, fish, and crayfish
This snake is disappearing from certain habitats in river areas of southern Arizona

Plains Blackhead Snake

Animal group: Reptile
Family: Colubrid snake – Size: 7–14½ ins
Feeds at night on centipedes, millipedes, spiders, and insects

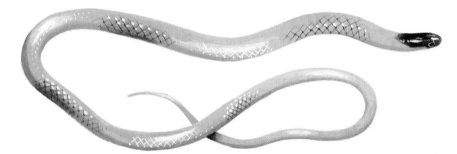

You will recognize this snake by its black head and white belly, which contrast with its unpatterned brownish gray body. This is a secretive snake that lives in prairies, desert grasslands, and woods in the southern Plains. It sometimes shelters in burrows, and often under flat rocks in hilly areas. The female lays clutches of 1 to 3 eggs in spring or summer.

Bullsnake

This powerfully built snake is usually yellowish with about forty brown blotches along its body. It is active during the day, and often shelters in the burrow of a mammal or tortoise at night. If confronted, a Bullsnake hisses loudly, then lunges at its intruder. Bullsnakes mate in spring, and lay up to twenty-four eggs in a burrow in sandy soil, or under a big rock or log. The young are about 12 to 18 inches long when they hatch.

Animal group: Reptile
Family: Colubrid snake
Size: 48–100 ins
Feeds mainly on rodents such as rats and mice

Great Plains Rat Snake

This secretive snake is related to the colorful Corn Snake, but is gray with brown blotches. It has a spearhead shape between its eyes and stripes under the tail. The Great Plains Rat Snake hides during the day under stones and in rock crevices, and comes out at night to hunt. They are found in rocky outcroppings and broken country in grassland areas.

Animal group: Reptile – Family: Colubrid snake
Size: 24–72 ins – Eats rats, mice, and birds
Also seen close to rivers, streams, meadows, abandoned buildings, and barns

Eastern Yellow-bellied Racer

With its green coloring, this snake is easily mistaken for a Smooth Green Snake, especially when young. It is a fast, agile snake that can climb well. It hunts for food during the day, and speeds along with its head held high off the ground. Like other racers, these snakes mate in spring and lay their eggs in summer under a rock or in a mammal burrow. Sometimes several females lay their eggs in the same nest. If annoyed, a Racer may act like a rattlesnake by rustling its tail in dead leaves to make a rattling sound. These snakes often hibernate in large groups.

Animal group: Reptile
Family: Colubrid snake
Size: 20–50 ins
Eats large insects, frogs, lizards, other snakes, rodents, and birds

Prairie Rattlesnake

This fierce and dangerous snake has two light lines on its head and blotches along its body. It lives in the grasslands of the Great Plains, and during the winter it shelters deep underground. It mates in spring and fall, and the female gives birth to between four and twenty-one young in late summer to fall.

Animal group: Reptile
Family: Pit viper
Size: 35–45 ins
Adults feed mostly on small mammals, including rodents and prairie dogs, and the young eat lizards and mice
WARNING: Avoid. Extremely dangerous

Western Box Turtle

This turtle has a hinged lower shell, so it can shut itself inside completely if danger threatens. You are most likely to find one in gently rolling prairies with sandy soil, especially on a sunny morning after rain. By midday, these turtles find a shady place to rest out of the sun. Look for disturbed piles of cow dung, as this is probably where a Box Turtle has been digging for beetles. The female lays 2 to 8 eggs in summer in a hole that she digs in the soil. The young hatch about ten weeks later. Male Box Turtles have red eyes and females have yellow-brown eyes.

Animal group: Reptile
Family: Pond, Marsh, and Box turtle
Shell size: 4–5 ins
Eats earthworms, caterpillars, grasshoppers, berries, leaves, and dead animals

Smooth Green Snake

Animal group: Reptile – Family: Colubrid snake – Size: 14–26 ins

You will need sharp eyesight to spy this beautiful, bright green snake as it slithers through the grass. It is small and streamlined, with a long tail, and is perfectly disguised in its grassland home. These snakes lay 3 to 11 eggs in late summer. Sometimes several females lay their eggs in the same place.

Tracks, Trails, & Calls

Dusk chorus

In Spring, keen bird watchers will be up at dawn to hear the "dawn chorus." Many birds sing enthusiastically at this time. If you go out at the other end of the day, just as the sun is setting, you may hear another chorus, this time made by frogs and toads. For instance, the chorus of the little Spring Peeper tree frog is familiar to many as among the first signs of spring.

In spring, the males of some species call so loudly they can be heard at least a mile away. They call to impress and attract females to mate with them. They also try to frighten smaller males with the loudness of their croak. The croak is made by pumping air in and out of a large balloon-like structure under the chin, called a "vocal sac."

Making recordings

Frogs and toads have distinctive calls. With practice, you can learn to identify the species just from its call. Try taking a small tape recorder out with you.

1 **Record the date, time and place** of your search on the tape.
2 **Track the animals down by following their croaks.** Move slowly and quietly, now and then stopping to listen.
3 **When you are quite near, record the sounds.**
4 **Now try to find the animals**. If you are lucky, you may catch a toad in the beam of your flashlight. Record on the tape which species you think it is; or describe what you see.

You can also buy tapes and learn from them. Newts and salamanders do not call, but many lizards do. Listen out for the calls of geckos. These range from cricket-like chirps to loud barks.

Making an impression

A good way to learn about animal tracks is to make a plaster-cast impression of them. Try making casts from pets' footprints and compare with those you find in the wild.

1 **Buy a bag of Plaster-of-Paris** from a drug store or craft shop.
2 **Cut out some strips of thin cardboard** about 12 inches long and 2 inches wide.

3 **Look for a clear footprint** preferably away from grass and other plants.
4 **Bend the card into a circle that will fit over the footprint**. Fix with a paper clip. For a long trail, try making an oblong shape.
5 **Push the card circle a little way down into the mud or sand.**
6 **Pour about 2 fl.oz of water into a jelly jar.** Add some Plaster-of-Paris and stir with a stick or old teaspoon. The mixture needs to be like thick cream. With practice, you will soon find out how much you need for a cast.

7 **Pour the mixture into your card circle** until it fills the footprint plus about $1/2$ inch on top.
8 **Leave it well alone until set.** This will take 15 to 20 minutes depending on the weather.
9 **Carefully prize up your cast** and peel off the cardboard surround.
10 **When the cast has dried out, brush off dirt with an old toothbrush.** You can paint the footprint and the surround in different colors. Remember, your cast will have lumps where the track had dents and vice versa!

Tracks & trails

The footprints of amphibians and reptiles are not as well known as those of mammals and birds. This is because many are too light to leave clear prints. But you can often tell what sort of animal has walked by, even if you can't tell the exact species. Learning to identify tracks and trails needs lots of practice. Look on page 79 for books which will help you.

Look in the mud around ponds for frog and toad tracks and turtle trails. In sandy areas and desert

country, look for lizard and sidewinder snake trails. Large tortoises leave clear footprints if they tread in mud or damp sand. Sea turtles leave wide, tank-like tracks on sandy beaches (look for them on the Florida and Gulf Coasts and beside tropical waters.)

Deserts & Arid Scrub

The hot, dry desert and scrub areas of the Southwest, where cactus, sagebrush, and creosote bushes grow, are the most difficult habitats for reptiles and amphibians to live in. Not many amphibians can stand the extreme heat and lack of water in a desert. Those that can survive in these conditions have developed special ways of keeping cool and moist. The Red-spotted Toad hides in deep crevices between rocks, while other toads escape from the heat by digging underground burrows. Here, they wait for a rainstorm which brings temporary pools for them to breed in.

A desert can sometimes be too hot for reptiles too. Snakes and lizards need the sun's heat to give them the energy to move, but even they may hide from the force of the midday sun in the burrow of a small mammal. Snakes and lizards, being cold-blooded, usually sunbathe in the morning until their body temperature reaches the correct level. They keep their body at the same temperature by moving in and out of the sun as they need to.

Most desert animals are active at night, when the temperature drops. A desert can become very cold at night, and keeping warm after sunset can be just as difficult as keeping cool during the day.

This picture shows six reptiles and amphibians from this book. How many do you recognize ?

Gila Monster (do not touch, its bite is poisonous), Leopard Lizard, Western Whiptail, Western Shovel-nosed Snake, Black-tailed Rattlesnake, Great Plains Narrow-mouthed Frog

Red-spotted Toad

It is quite easy to recognize this toad by the red or orange warts on its gray, orange, or reddish brown back. The Red-spotted Toad has a flat body and a pointed snout. It is the only North American toad that lays its eggs one at a time, at the bottom of a puddle. You are most likely to see these toads in shady canyons, moist stream edges, and mountains from the southern plains to California. They can climb well and usually shelter in cracks and crevices in rocks near an area of water such as a desert stream. They breed from March to September, during or after a storm. Listen for the males calling to the females. They make a high-pitched trilling sound.

Animal group: Amphibian
Family: Toad
Size: 1½–3 ins
Eats insects and other small invertebrates

Great Plains Narrow-mouthed Frog

This small, secretive frog usually hides during the day in a burrow or under bark or rocks, and is difficult to spot because it is so small. These frogs are plump and egg-shaped, with smooth skin. They have a small head with a pointed snout, and a fold of loose skin across the back of the head. There is a spade shape on each back foot, and no webbing between the toes. The males make a high-pitched buzzing sound. In the distance they sound like a flock of sheep, but up close they sound more like bees. These frogs breed from March to September when there are heavy desert rains, and the females lay their eggs on the surface of pools. The young have a leaf pattern on their backs, which disappears as they grow older and paler. This frog often shares the burrow of a mole, lizard, or even a tarantula.

Animal group: Amphibian
Family: Frog
Size: 1–1¾ ins
Eats insects, especially ants and termites
WARNING: Wash your hands well if you handle this frog. They produce a toxic substance that can burn if it gets into your eyes or mouth

Desert Tortoise

This is the only large, land-dwelling tortoise in its range – the deserts of southern California, Nevada, and Arizona. It is quite easy to recognize a Desert Tortoise because the lower part of its shell sticks out at the front below its throat. This tortoise has stubby hind legs and flattened front legs, which help it to dig. Look for tortoise tracks, which are rows of dents on sandy soil. Tortoises shelter from the sun at the hottest time of the day in a shallow burrow, often at the base of a creosote bush. In the early morning and late afternoon, when it is cooler, they venture out to feed. They mate in spring, and the female lays 2 to 14 eggs in a funnel-shaped nest. The young hatch in August to October and can live for more than twenty years. Sometimes these tortoises gather together in the fall and hibernate for the winter in an underground den.

Animal group: Reptile – Family: Tortoise – Shell size: 9¹/₄–15 ins
Eats grasses, herbs, and cacti – This is an endangered species

Couch's Spadefoot

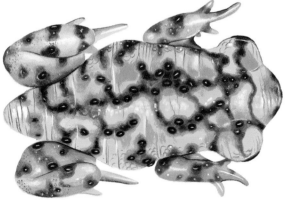

Animal group: Amphibian – Family: Spadefoot Toad
Size: 2¹/₄–3¹/₂ ins – Feeds on insects at night

This plump, round toad is yellow with blotches of black or dark green. It has smoother skin than many other toads. You can recognize a Couch's Spadefoot by its call, a sound like a lamb bleating. These toads live in deserts where creosote bushes grow, and also in savannahs and dry prairies. They mate from April to September, after heavy rain. The female lays her eggs on plant stems in puddles. The eggs develop quickly, and the tadpoles hatch after only thirty-six hours. They grow into adults within 2 to 6 weeks, before the desert sun dries up all the pools. During the hottest time of day, and in very dry weather, this toad hides from the sun in the burrow of a small mammal, or it digs itself a hole in the sandy soil.

Deserts & Arid Scrub

Banded Gecko

This lizard is a light tan colour with dark bands or blotches and protruding eyelids. Look for it in sand dunes and canyons, often near rocks. It hides in cracks and crevices at the hottest times of the day, and comes out at night to hunt. When it is hunting, it swishes its tail just like a cat. These lizards look very delicate with their soft skin, but they can survive in the very dry deserts. If you want to find one, look during the spring, before the ground is too hot. These lizards lay 1 to 3 clutches of two eggs from May to September, and the hatchlings appear about forty-five days later.

Animal group: Reptile
Family: Gecko
Size: 4–6 ins
Eats spiders and insects

Desert Iguana

The Desert Iguana is a large, light-colored lizard that scurries away to hide at the slightest hint of danger, sometimes running on its hind legs. Iguanas enjoy the heat of the desert, and you might see one basking in the sun on a rock, close to a burrow for safety. They are often out in the sun when other lizards are sheltering. If the ground becomes too hot, they climb up into a bush where it is cooler. These lizards mate in April to May and lay 3 to 8 eggs in June to August, which hatch between August and September. Desert Iguanas are most common in rocky, sandy habitats in California, Nevada, and western Arizona, into Mexico.

Animal group: Reptile – Family: Iguanid – Size: 10–16 ins
Eats mainly the leaves, buds, and flowers of desert vegetation, as well as insects, small lizards, and sometimes dead animals

Leopard Lizard

Animal group: Reptile
Family: Iguanid
Size: 8¹/₂–15 ins
Eats insects and smaller lizards

This gray or brown spotted lizard is found in sandy or gravelly areas of the southwestern U.S. The Leopard Lizard is very agile and will lie in wait in the shade, darting out to catch any passing prey. They lay 4 to 7 eggs between May and July, sometimes with a second batch later in the summer.

Gila Monster

The Gila Monster is the only poisonous lizard in the U.S. When it bites its victim, venom is produced by glands in its jaw and flows through grooves in its teeth while it chews its prey. You can recognize the Gila Monster by the tiny orange and black scales all over its body, and by the way it flicks its forked tongue in and out like a snake. It has a large head, a heavy body, and a thick tail where fat is stored for times when food is in short supply. Gila Monsters live in shrubby, grassy desert on the slopes of mountains and in canyons. They dig burrows or use the burrows of other animals for shelter. Gila Monsters mate during the summer and females lay 3 to 5 eggs in fall or winter.

Animal group: Reptile – Family: Gila monster – Size: 18–24 ins
Preys at night on small mammals and also
bird and reptile eggs
This is an endangered species
WARNING: If you find a Gila Monster, do not handle it. These lizards have a hard, poisonous bite that is extremely painful.

Chuckwalla

The Chuckwalla looks rather fat around the middle, has a tapering tail and what looks like wrinkles of skin on its shoulders. It is active during the day, but before it does anything at all the chuckwalla has to raise its body temperature and that requires sunbathing for an hour or two. Chuckwallas live near rocky hillsides where creosote bushes grow. Look for long, pellet-shaped droppings containing plant fibers. You may find some near a Chuckwalla's favorite sunbathing spot or hiding place. This lizard has an extraordinary way of defending itself. If alarmed, the Chuckwalla dashes into a crevice and gulps air to puff out its body so that it is wedged in and cannot be pulled out. Listen for a scratching sound a bit like sandpaper – it might be a Chuckwalla scuttling into a crevice. Female Chuckwallas lay 5 to 10 eggs in June to August every other year.

Animal group: Reptile – Family: Iguanid
Size: 11–16½ ins – Eats plants

Desert Spiny Lizard

You can recognize this stocky lizard by the black, wedge-shaped mark on each side of its neck and the pointed scales that cover its body, which look like rose thorns. The male has a blue-green patch on his throat and on each side of his belly. The Desert Spiny Lizard is very shy and darts for cover in a crevice if frightened. It lives in areas where Joshua trees, creosote bushes, and juniper grow, and it is a good climber. These lizards are active by day and shelter at night under logs, rocks, and in the nests of rats and other rodents. They mate in early summer and lay 4 to 19 eggs in May to June.

Animal group: Reptile – Family: Iguanid – Size: 7–12 ins
Feeds on insects and occasionally
flowers and leaves

Texas Horned Lizard

This round, flat-bodied lizard is easy to spot by the ring of thorny spines on its head. The two larger center spines help to protect it from attackers. Two rows of spines along the body and mottled camouflage colors help to protect it, too. These lizards are also called "horned toads" because their flattened shape makes them look like toads. The Horned Lizard is active during the warmest part of the day and can run fast. When it is not active, it hides in mammal burrows, clumps of vegetation, or lies just under the surface of the sand with only its head above ground. You may be lucky enough to see one in rocky, sandy, arid areas of the southern Plains, from Kansas to southeast Arizona and Texas. Like other horned lizards, this lizard has an extraordinary way of putting off attackers. If threatened, it may squirt a stream of blood from its eyes, which can reach several feet away. Despite its thorns and camouflage colors, this lizards is preyed on by birds such as roadrunners, and by other reptiles, including collared lizards.

Animal group: Reptile
Family: Iguanid
Size: 2$\frac{1}{2}$–7$\frac{1}{4}$ ins
Feeds on large ants and other insects
These lizards are now protected by law in many states

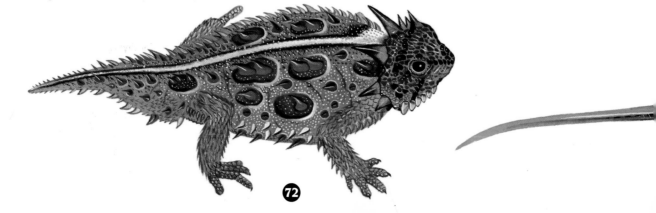

Western Whiptail

There are many kinds of whiptails in the Americas, and you can easily spot them by their jerky way of moving. They run fast, turning their head from side to side as they go, sticking out their forked tongue. The Western Whiptail stalks its prey like a cat, and also stalks any other moving objects, including fluttering leaves. These lizards live in deserts and semi-deserts where there are hardly any plants, and they prefer open places. A Whiptail may allow you to sneak up on it for a closer look, but it usually stays out of reach, then dashes for cover when you get too close. They sometimes shelter in the burrow of another animal. Whiptails lay 1 to 3 clutches of 1 to 8 eggs in April and August. Some kinds of Whiptail produce only female young.

Animal group: Reptile
Family: Whiptail lizard – Size: 8–12 ins
Hunts spiders, scorpions, insects, and other lizards
Also lives in pine forests and woodland.

Sagebrush Lizard

This spiny lizard has pointed, overlapping scales and faint stripes running along its back. The males usually have a mottled, light blue pattern on the throat and dark blue patches on the belly. Females have pinkish orange on their neck and sides. Sagebrush Lizards are a common sight in sandy, gravelly areas where sagebrush grows. They spend most of their time on the ground, but sometimes climb trees in search of insects. They never wander far from a place to shelter and, if alarmed, they hide in bushes, among rocks, or up a tree. Sagebrush Lizards lay one to two clutches of two to seven eggs in early summer, which hatch about a month later. They are found in sage flats and mountains from the western Plains to California and central Washington.

Animal group: Reptile
Family: Iguanid
Size: 5–6 ins
Hunts for insects, spiders, mites, ticks, and scorpions in the morning, after basking in the sun

Side-blotched Lizard

You are most likely to see these lizards in semi-desert areas from Texas to southern California and as far north as central Washington. They live in various habitats, including sandy and rocky areas where there are few trees, shrubs, and grasses. The Side-blotched Lizard has small, smooth scales with no spines, and is so named because of the blue or black blotch on each side of its chest behind its front legs. These lizards spend most of their time on the ground, so look for them near low-growing bushes. In the warm South, they are active all year round, and lay 2 to 7 clutches of between 1 and 8 eggs. In the cooler north, they are not active in winter, and lay 1 to 3 clutches of between 1 and 5 eggs.

Animal group: Reptile – Family: Iguanid – Size: 4–6½ ins
Feeds on insects, spiders, scorpions, ticks, mites, and other bugs

Western Patch-nosed Snake

This slim-bodied snake can be seen during the day hunting for lizards, mice, and young snakes. Western Patch-nosed Snakes live in deserts and semi-desert areas where creosote and sagebrushes grow, and you may spot one sunbathing on a rock. They have smooth scales, and are gray or a muddy tan with a wide yellowish stripe along the top of the body and darker stripes along each side. The females lay between 4 and 10 eggs during the summer months, and the young hatch after two or three months.

Animal group: Reptile
Family: Colubrid snake
Size: 2–4 ft long

Glossy Snake

Glossy Snakes vary in color from faded pink to cream or light brown with brown, gray, or tan marks rimmed with black. Their scales look shiny. Look for the dark line running from the jaw to the corner of the eye. These snakes are active mainly at night, and you may see one on a summer's evening, especially in open, sandy desert areas where creosote and sagebrush grow. Glossy Snakes live in southeast Texas, southeast Nebraska, central California, and south into Mexico. They mate in spring and lay a clutch of up to 23 eggs in summer. Glossy Snakes are sometimes nicknamed "faded snakes" because of their pale coloring.

Animal group: Reptile – Family: Colubrid snake
Size: 2–6 ft long
Eats lizards and sometimes small mammals

Desert Kingsnake

You are most likely to see this large, brown snake early in the morning or at dusk, when it is most active. In the hottest months of the year it finds shelter during the day and hunts at night. Kingsnakes are powerful constrictors. They feed on lizards, rodents and birds, and also eat other snakes, including the poisonous rattlesnakes and coral snakes. They are able to eat these snakes because they are immune to snake venom. Kingsnakes mate in March to June and lay up to 24 creamy white eggs in May to August.

Animal group: Reptile
Family: Colubrid Snake
Size: 3–7 ft long

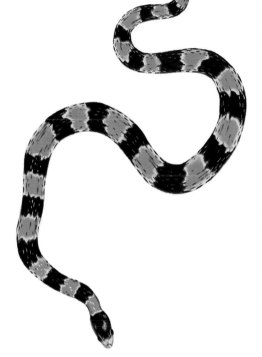

Sonora Gopher Snake

This big, powerful snake has a pointed snout and blotches of reddish brown on the front part of its body. Sonora Gopher Snakes are out and about during the day, but those living in very hot deserts are also active at night. Sonora Gopher Snakes mate in spring and lay up to 24 creamy white eggs in June to August. They are good at burrowing, and may lay their eggs in a burrow in sandy soil. Sometimes they shelter in the burrow of a tortoise or rodent, or under a rock. If threatened, this snake hisses loudly, raises its head, vibrates its tail, then strikes.

Animal group: Reptile
Family: Colubrid snake
Size: 4–8 ft long
Eats mice and other
small mammals, and
also birds' eggs

Long-nosed Snake

This colorful, smooth-skinned snake has bands of red, black and yellowish cream. You can recognize a Long-nosed Snake by its long, pointed snout which sticks out further than the lower jaw. Long-nosed Snakes are active at night and spend the day sheltering under a rock or in a burrow. They are found in the deserts and dry prairies of the extreme Southwest. They mate in spring and lay 4 to 9 eggs in a burrow in June to August. The young hatch after two or three months.

Animal group: Reptile
Family: Colubrid snake
Size: 2–4 ft long
Eats lizards and their eggs,
small rodents, and small snakes

Deserts & Arid Scrub

Western Diamondback Rattlesnake

This is the biggest of all the rattlesnakes, and probably the most dangerous snake in North America. If threatened, this snake stands its ground, lifting its head high and rattling its tail. Like all rattlesnakes, the Western Diamondback has curved fangs at the front of its upper jaw, which swing forward to strike at prey as the snake opens its mouth. These rattlesnakes are active at the end of the day and at night during the summer, and hunt birds, rodents, rabbits, and lizards. They live in rocky canyons, brushy desert, and also in mountain areas. They mate in late March to May and also in fall, and the females give birth to 4 to 25 young in late summer. The young can be up to 13 inches long at birth. They can live for more than 25 years. This snake is nicknamed "Coontail Rattler" because its tail has black and white or light gray rings like a racoon's tail.

Animal group: Reptile
Family: Pit Viper – Size: 3–7 ft long

WARNING: Avoid— EXTREMELY POISONOUS!
This snake's bite can kill you

Western Shovel-nosed Snake

Brightly striped like a wasp, this snake is very striking. It is usually yellow or white with 21 or more dark brown or black bands. Sometimes the bands are reddish orange in color. The Western Shovel-nosed Snake has a flattened snout that sticks out above the lower jaw. Its flattened body, smooth scales, and an ability to close its nostrils enable it to burrow into sand easily and speedily. It is active mainly at night and feeds on insects, spiders, scorpions, and centipedes. This snake can live in the driest deserts, where there are hardly any plants. It usually stays underground by day and comes out at night when the temperature is cooler. You may spot one crossing a highway, especially in Nevada, Baja California, and Mexico.

Animal group: Reptile – Family: Colubrid snake
Size: 10–17 ins long – Lays 2 to 4 eggs in the summer

Night Snake

This snake lives in all sorts of habitats, from deserts to grasslands, to mountain meadows and woodlands, both in rocky and sandy places. But you will be lucky to see one because Night Snakes hide by day under rocks, in crevices, and under fallen branches. They come out at night to hunt for frogs, lizards, and salamanders. Look out for one crossing a highway during the evening. Night Snakes are pale gray or light brown with gray or brown blotches on the back and sides. There are usually two large, dark brown blotches on the neck. The head is flattish, and the scales are smooth. The females lay 2 to 9 eggs between April and August.

Animal group: Reptile
Family: Colubrid snake
Size: 1–2 ft long

One of the most colorful snakes in the world is also one of the deadliest. The Arizona Coral Snake is easy to spot by its striking red, yellow, and black bands, but it is also easy to mistake it for the harmless Milk Snake, which looks very similar. Coral Snakes live in rocky desert areas in central Arizona to southwest New Mexico and into Mexico. These glossy-skinned snakes usually shelter in a burrow by day and venture out by night to hunt for small snakes, especially during or after a shower of rain. The females lay 2 or 3 eggs in late summer. If a Coral Snake is threatened by a predator, it hides its head in its coils and shows the underside of its tail to frighten the attacker away.

Arizona Coral Snake

Animal group: Reptile
Family: Elapidae/Coral Snake
Size: 1–2 ft long
WARNING: Avoid—EXTREMELY POISONOUS! This snake's bite can kill you. Remember that "red-yellow-black" means danger!

Black-tailed Rattlesnake

This snake is quite easy to recognize by its black tail, which contrasts with the rest of the body. The Black-tailed Rattlesnake is patterned with black or brown blotches on olive, gray, cream, or tan. Sometimes the markings on its back are diamond-shaped. Black-tailed Rattlesnakes are active during the day and night, especially after rain. The females give birth to between 3 and 6 live young during the summer. You are most likely to see one of these snakes in Arizona, central Texas, or central Mexico. They are not found in barren desert, and are more common in rocky, mountainous areas. This rattlesnake is not as aggressive as other rattlers, but it is still very dangerous—keep away from it.

Animal group: Reptile
Family: Pit Viper
Size: 28–48 ins long
WARNING: Avoid—EXTREMELY POISONOUS!
This snake's bite can kill you

Sidewinder

This desert rattlesnake is easy to recognize by the "horns" above each eye. These horns act like sunshades to protect the snake's eyes from the desert sun and allow it to spy its prey. As their name suggests, Sidewinders move in an S-shaped curve. Winding sideways is a fast and efficient way of traveling on hot sand, and the snake's body hardly touches the ground. Look for the J-shaped tracks of a Sidewinder. The hooked part of the "J" shows you the direction that the snake was going. Sidewinders are usually found close to the burrows of rodents, especially where creosote bushes grow. They are active mainly at night and usually spend the day sheltering in the burrow of another animal. Sometimes a Sidewinder rests in a shallow pit in the shade of a shrub. The females give birth to 5 to 18 live young in late summer or early fall.

Animal group: Reptile
Family: Pit Viper – Size: 12–35 ins
Eats birds and rodents such as pocket mice and kangaroo rats – WARNING:
Avoid—EXTREMELY POISONOUS! This snake's bite can kill you

Find Out Some More

Useful Organizations

People who study amphibians and reptiles are called herpetologists (say it: *her-per-tol-loh-jist*.) In addition to the national groups listed below, most states have their own herpetological society, and there are hundreds of local natural history associations. Check with your teacher, or with your nearest natural history museum, wildlife refuge, or local public library for information on them.

Society for the Study of Amphibians and Reptiles is the best group for you to contact. Write to: Society for the Study of Amphibians and Reptiles, c/o Dr. Douglas Taylor, Miami University, Dept. of Zoology, Oxford, Ohio 45056.

On the East Coast, you should contact the **New England Herpetological Society**. Write to: New England Herpetological Society, P.O. Box 082, Boston, Massachusetts 02103.

On the West Coast, contact the **Herpetologist's League**. Write to: Herpetologist's League, Texas Natural Heritage Program, Texas Parks & Wildlife Department, 3000 Interstate Highway 5, Suite 100, Austin, Texas 78704.

The **American Society of Ichthyology and Herpetology** is a group for professional zoologists and serious amateurs (ichthyology is the study of fish.) Write to: American Society of Ichthyology and Herpetology, Department of Zoology, Business Office, Southern Illinois University, Carbondale, Illinois 62901–6501.

Reptile and Amphibian Magazine is published every second month. To subscribe to it, write to: Reptile and Amphibian Magazine, RD#3, Box 3709–A, Pottsville, Pennsylvania 17901.

Many of the preserves owned by the **Nature Conservancy** and its chapters conserve unique and threatened habitats for amphibians and reptiles. Write to: Nature Conservancy, Suite 800, 1800 North Kent Street, Arlington, Virginia 22209.

In Canada, the **Canadian Nature Foundation** is a good starting point. Write to: Canadian Nature Foundation, 453 Sussex Drive, Ottawa, Ontario K1N 6Z4.

Places To Visit

Back Bay National Wildlife Refuge, Virginia Beach, Virginia. Tidal marshes, freshwater ponds, and brackish (slightly salty) ponds are homes for snapping turtles, mud turtles, and other species.

Everglades National Park, Flamingo, South Florida. This "river of grass" is the home of water snakes, American alligators, cottonmouths, softshell turtles, plus many other amphibians.

Corkscrew Swamp Sanctuary, Naples, Florida. Owned by the National Audubon Society, there is a two-mile-long boardwalk through the cypress swamps where you may see tree lizards, American alligators, and a wide variety of snakes.

Great Smoky Mountains National Park, Tennessee–North Carolina. This is the home of 28 different species of salamander—North America's largest collection. The moist forests shelter over 120 species of amphibians and reptiles.

Big Bend National Park, Texas. Nearly a million acres of Chihuahuan Desert are home to many desert species, including horned lizards, rattlesnakes, and geckos. The Rio Grande River provides a home for many amphibians including the canyon treefrog and the leopard frog.

Wind Cave National Park, Hot Springs, South Dakota. Best known for its cave system, this is an area where grassland and Rocky Mountains forests meet. Look for northern Plains species like the Great Plains toad, western hognose snake, yellow-bellied racer, and western rattlesnake.

There are also many preserves and sanctuaries in every state—check with your teacher, your nearest natural history museum, wildlife refuge, or local public library for information on them.

Index & Glossary

To find the name of an animal in this index, search under its main name. So, to look up Eastern Box Turtle; look under Turtle, Box, not under Eastern.

Useful Books

Amazing Frogs & Toads, Barry Clarke (Eyewitness Juniors, Alfred A. Knopf).
Amazing Snakes, Alexandra Parsons (Eyewitness Juniors, Alfred A. Knopf).
Audubon Society Field Guide to North American Reptiles and Amphibians, John L. Behler & F. Wayne King (Alfred A. Knopf). A photographic guide that describes all the species found in North America north of Mexico.
Encyclopedia of Reptiles and Amphibians, Dr. Tim Halliday & Dr. Kraig Adler (Facts on File). Detailed information about species around the world.
A Guide to Amphibians and Reptiles, Thomas F. Tyning (Little, Brown Co.). In-depth information on the lives of thirty-two common species.
Peterson First Guide to Reptiles and Amphibians (Houghton Mifflin Co.). A simplified pocket-sized guide to common species.

Index & Glossary

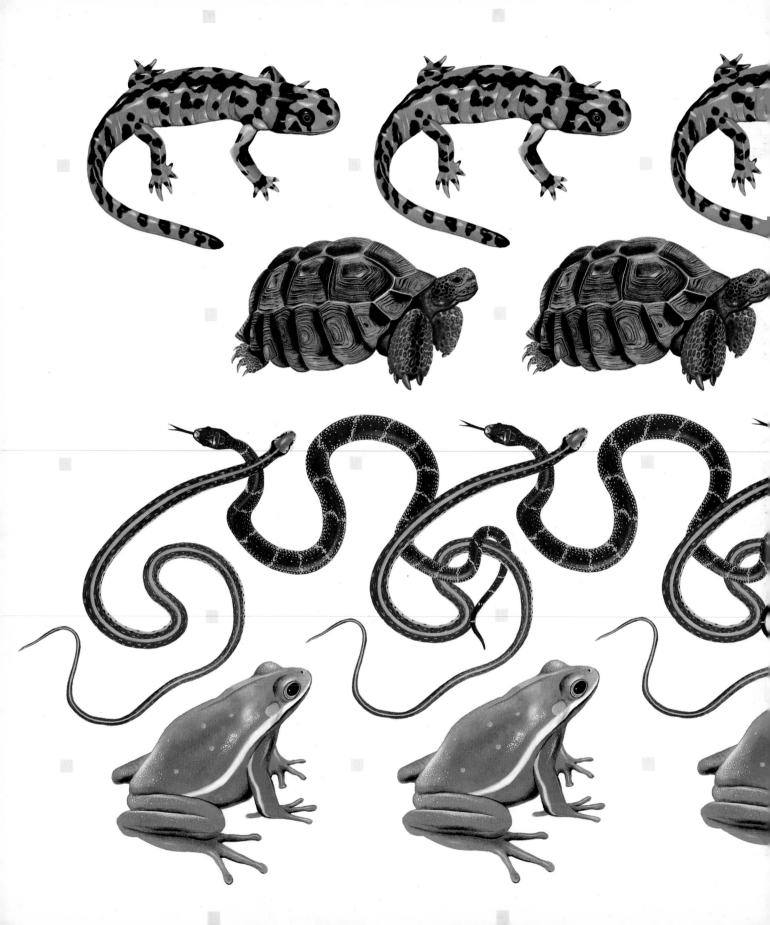